REASONS *of the* HEART

REASONS
of the
HEART

A vision for the new millennium

BRUCE WILSON

ALLEN & UNWIN
AND
ALBATROSS BOOKS

First published in 1998 by
Allen & Unwin
9 Atchison Street,
St Leonards NSW 1590
Australia
Phone: (61 2) 8425 0100
Fax: (61 2) 9906 2218
E-mail: frontdesk@allen-unwin.com.au
Web: http://www.allen-unwin.com.au

Albatross Books
PO Box 320, Sutherland NSW 2232
Australia
Fax: (61 2) 9521 1515
E-mail: albatross@albatross.com.au
Web: http://www.publishaustralia.com.au

National Library of Australia
Cataloguing-in-Publication entry:

Wilson, Bruce, 1942– .
    Reasons of the heart: a vision for the new millennium.

    ISBN 1 86448 900 6.

    1. Christianity. 2. Experience (Religion). 3. Spiritual life. I. Title.

248

Printed by Australian Print Group, Maryborough, Victoria

10 9 8 7 6 5 4 3 2 1

Contents

Introduction

SERIOUS MODERN FILM CREATES MANY OF THE TRUE myths of our time. It refuses to bow to the rigid and arid scientific orthodoxy that has entrapped our culture and sucks away at its humanistic and spiritual life-blood, attempting to reduce us and our world to its quantitative abstractions. All that is— visible and invisible, the human soul and its life-world— contains a plethora of riches, subtlety and freedom never to be grasped by mere abstraction and quantification.

With sensitive panache, modern film, pushing its artistic imagination almost past the impossible, continues to explore the great questions:

- What is this being human?
- What is love?
- What is evil?
- How is a human life fulfilled?
- What is transcendence?
- How does meaning come?
- Where is grace?

Since completing the last chapter of this book, in which I explore Kryzstof Kieslowski's film trilogy *Three Colours: Blue, White* and *Red,*

I have seen Lars Von Trier's latest film, *Breaking the Waves*. And what a harrowing and enriching experience that was!

Von Trier just barely avoids going right over the top as he portrays through Bess, the main character, the contradictory extremes of our modern psyche and culture. Condensed in Bess are all our current tensions of sanity and madness, of sexuality with and without love, of religious power to fortify or to destroy us, of freedom and of social conformity, of the damnation of our souls or their salvation through grace.

In cultural terms, I sometimes wonder whether those under fifty would possess any spiritual hope were it not for some of today's great film-makers. Film's resurgent popularity is most to be understood, I think, as youth's search for meaning through great and true myths.

My own life is rooted deeply in the spiritual tradition founded by Jesus Christ. It delights me to see so many modern film-makers drawing at the water-wells of this tradition for truth to live by. But it saddens me that the church of the West, except in shallow, fundamentalistic forms, seems less and less able to portray with winsomeness its own true myth to the current generations.

This book is written in the hope that something of the Spirit of Jesus will prove seductive for those who seek truly transforming and life-giving experiences. For we know that we cannot live by bread alone, nor by bread and circuses.

My thanks sincerely to the following people (in alphabetical order) for their help, their critical comments and their encouragement in the process of writing this book:

Michael Godfrey
Jonathan Heasman

Norman Kempson
Aniko Koro
Donald Meadows
Ingrid Pulley
Allan Reeder
Andrew Smith
Anthea Wilson
Richard Wilson
Zandra Wilson

Where personal stories of living individuals are told in this book, appropriate details have been altered to ensure anonymity.

PART A:

OUT OF THE CLOSET

1.

Theophany

Mud, meteorites and
mystical intelligence

I F WE ARE ILL, MOST OF US FEEL RELIEF WHEN THE DOCTOR
puts a name to our ailment. Not knowing what we've got can be
as unbearable as the illness itself. Diagnostic naming can lift a veil
of fear, even if the illness is serious.

The ancients recognised this power of naming. They believed
we could not control an evil influence, a demon, until we found
out its name. Sometimes, the absence of a name results in
non-recognition of experiences we actually do have. 'Homophobia' and 'theophany' are striking examples.

Not more than five years ago, an intelligent, educated colleague
asked me, 'What's homophobia?' Today, even schoolchildren know
the meaning of this word. But how many of us recognised our
psychological fear of homosexuality or homosexuals before it was
given a name? The fear was always there, recognition of it was not.
To consciously feel or talk about the fear was a forbidden experience.

✠ Theophany, a forbidden experience

How many of us experience theophany, but do not consciously
recognise it or talk about it? Such talk is still a forbidden

experience. If we try, we are quickly ostracised as strange or odd, so we have learnt to keep our theophanies in the closet.

If I were playing it safe, I would say that most people experience theophany. For reasons which will gradually unfold, I would rather not play it safe and say instead that *everyone* experiences it. Yet, as we shall see, even eminent people succumb to social pressure and keep quiet about their theophanies.

I am writing this book in the hope that it will help remove theophany from the realm of forbidden experience and forbidden public talk. In modern society, so strong is the pressure to keep the experience in the closet that the word itself, like 'lesbian' in the Victorian era, has just about dropped out of our language.

The word 'theophany' means a manifestation or appearance of God to a human being. But the best way to understand it is to hear the stories people tell about their experiences.

✠ Patrick White's theophany

Patrick White is the only Australian to win the Nobel Prize for literature. Until late in life, he kept his experience of theophany in the closet— as he did his homosexuality. He knew both were deviant from the social mainstream.

Awareness of God came to him by theophany in 1951 when he was nearly forty. He did not speak about it publicly until the publication of his self-portrait, *Flaws in the Glass*, thirty years later in 1981. His spiritual reticence in the face of hostility is apparent in a letter he wrote in 1969 to his friend Maie Casey, wife of the then Australian Governor-General, about the painter Sidney Nolan:

> I am always a bit uneasy when painters start painting flowers
> and poets write about birds; I feel they are avoiding the more

important things they should be doing. When we met in San Francisco last year, I felt Sid was a bit lost: he'd been hit by the present trend in painting and didn't quite know where to go next. I had to try to tell him I was altogether lost and just intended to go where I was led by whatever leads me (God, of course; though it hardly does to go around saying it directly).[1]

Theophanies may be ordinary or they may be dramatic and visionary. White's was ordinary. It occurred when he and his lifetime partner, Manoly Lascaris, were living on a farmlet at Castle Hill on Sydney's outskirts. White explains what happened:

During what seemed like months of rain, I was carrying a trayload of food to a wormy litter of pups down at the kennels when I slipped and fell on my back, dog dishes shooting in all directions. I lay where I had fallen, half-blinded by rain, under a pale sky, cursing through watery lips a God in whom I did not believe. I began laughing, finally, at my own helplessness and hopelessness, in the mud and stench from my filthy old oilskin. It was the turning point. My disbelief appeared as farcical as my fall. At that moment, I was truly humbled.[2]

Prior to this slip-in-the-mud theophany, White says he believed in nothing but his own egotism and 'in my own brash godhead'.[3] After it, he and Manoly began attending worship each Sunday at Castle Hill Anglican Church. Their attendance ceased 'after the rector of the day declared it sinful to guess the number of beans in a jar at the annual church fete'.[4]

Following an aborted attempt to discover a more congenial place of worship, White says: 'Each of us retreated into his private faith and there we have remained.'[5]

It was retreat from institutional religion, not God. White came to view his novels as the artistic expression of the reality he experienced with his slip-in-the-mud theophany:

> I suppose what I am increasingly intent on doing in my books is to give professed unbelievers glimpses of their own unprofessed faith. I believe most people have a religious faith, but are afraid that by admitting it they will forfeit their right to be considered intellectuals.[6]

A seminal influence on Patrick White's later spiritual outlook was the American Trappist monk and mystical writer extraordinaire, Thomas Merton.

✠ Some of Thomas Merton's theophanies

Merton did not grow up in a religious family. Religion figured in Merton's childhood negatively, through an influential anti-Catholic grandfather. His early life as an adult was artistic, intellectual and given over to much drunkenness and womanising.

Merton's theophanic awakenings reflect his character and come in distinct stages. The first occurred after the death of his father when he was just eighteen, an event that evoked a new reflectiveness about life itself and the direction of his own moral behaviour:

> I was in my room. It was night. The light was on. Suddenly, it seemed to me that Father, who had now been dead more than a year, was there with me. The sense of his presence was as vivid and as real and as startling as if he had touched my arm or spoken to me.
>
> The whole thing passed in a flash, but in that flash,

instantly, I was overwhelmed with a sudden and profound insight into the misery and corruption of my own soul, and I was pierced deeply with a light that made me realise something of the condition I was in . . . my soul desired escape and liberation and freedom from all this with an intensity and an urgency unlike anything I had ever known before.

And now I think for the first time in my whole life I really began to pray . . . praying out of the very roots of my life and of my being, and praying to the God I had never known, to reach down towards me out of his darkness.[7]

It was as a student at Columbia University in New York that Merton had his second significant theophany, an awakening of mind to God centred on the one word 'aseity'. He had enrolled in a course on mediaeval French literature, during which he purchased and read Etienne Gilson's book, *The Spirit of Mediaeval Philosophy*. To this point, there was no marriage between Merton's direct spiritual experience and mental vision.

Though we do not know for certain, until he discovered *aseity* he appears to have been puzzled by an immature image of God epitomised by the school pupil's and undergraduate's question: 'If God created the universe, who created God?' 'Aseity' answered this question and answered it in a way that made sense of his earlier nascent mysticism and his later profound experiences:

In this one word, which can be applied to God alone and which expresses his most characteristic attribute, I discovered an entirely new concept of God, a concept which showed me at once that the belief of Catholics was by no means the vague and rather superstitious hangover from an unscientific age that I had believed it to be. On the contrary, here was a notion of God that was at the same time deep, precise, simple and accurate and, what is more, charged with implications which I could not even begin to appreciate . . .

'Aseitas' simply means the power of a being to exist absolutely in virtue of itself, not as caused by itself, but as requiring no cause, no other justification for its existence except that its very nature is to exist. There can be only one such Being: that is God. And to say that God exists *a se*, of and by reason of himself, is merely to say that God is Being itself. *Ego sum qui sum* ('I am who I am') . . .

This notion made such a profound impression on me that I made a pencil note at the top of the page: 'Aseity of God—God is Being *per se*.' [8]

By 1938, Merton had graduated and begun work on a postgraduate thesis on 'Nature and Art in William Blake'. He was smoking an enormous number of cigarettes each day, 'got plastered', as he said, fairly regularly and pursued women with his accustomed excess.

His third crucial theophany was a theophany of the inner voice. On a Sunday just previous to it—the first time, he notes, he had ever spent a sober Sunday in New York—he went to church. He had become entranced with the writings of the Catholic poet Gerard Manley Hopkins and one night, whilst reading Hopkins, came the critical turning point of his spiritual life:

'What are you waiting for?' said the voice within me . . .
'Why are you sitting there? It is useless to hesitate any longer. Why don't you get up and go?' . . .
. . . Suddenly, I could bear it no longer. I put down the book, got into my raincoat and started down the stairs. I went out into the street. I crossed over and went along by

the gray wooden fence, towards Broadway, in the light rain.

And then everything inside me began to sing . . . I had nine blocks to walk. Then, I turned the corner of 121st Street, and the brick church and presbytery were before me. I stood in the doorway and rang the bell and waited. When the maid opened the door, I said: 'May I see Father Ford, please?'

'But Father Ford is out.' . . . The maid closed the door. I stepped back into the street. And then I saw Father Ford coming around the corner from Broadway . . .

I went to meet him and said: 'Father, may I speak to you about something?'

'Yes,' he said, looking up, surprised. 'Yes, sure, come into the house.'

We sat in the little parlor by the door. And I said: 'Father, I want to become a Catholic.' [9]

Whether a theophany is ordinary, or whether it is dramatic and visionary, usually has more to do with the way the story is told than with the actual experience. Neither White's nor Merton's inner experience was ordinary. Both were awakened to a dimension that is definitely not ordinary to secular mentality, to God and the spiritual. In both cases—a slip in the mud, a word in a book—the outer experiences were mundane.

✠ Some personal theophanies

One of my own theophanies could be told in the most dramatic and visionary way if the outer experience were emphasised at the expense of the inner.

Like Merton, I did not grow up in a religious family. I accepted God in my youth at high school, aged seventeen, as a result of two things. First, I became convinced intellectually that it was possible to believe in the theory of evolution *and* in divine creation. Previously, I had dismissed the possibility of God, in my head at least, because I held that science had exposed the idea of creation as a biblical and religious fairytale.

Second, I saw in three men I knew a depth and integrity of person which was absent from my own life. Even with decades of hindsight behind me, I cannot put into precise words what it actually was I saw in them. It was as though each had a light glowing in his dark soul whilst my soul was a mere shadow, without substance or contrast.

One was an active practising Catholic, another a Baptist and the third an Anglican. Words such as 'purpose', 'strength' and 'honour' and phrases such as 'love for others' and 'high sense of justice' come to mind as I think of them. They were my theophany of spiritual awakening. God appeared palpable to me in the lives of these three otherwise quite ordinary human beings. There was nothing dramatic and visionary about it.

It is my original sense of call to the ordained ministry that is capable of a dramatic and visionary interpretation. I hesitate to tell the story at all because I was so young. Initially, it will sound quite silly, if not plain ridiculous. For over thirty years I have kept it to myself because I know it is open to scathing ridicule.

I tell it now because I have come to realise that the young experience profoundly and deeply, whether that experience is of love or of suffering or of spirituality. I tell it, too, because I suspect it will have resonances for other adults who have either negated or suppressed their youthful experiences when what is needed is mature interpretation of a possibly valid core. I also tell it because, even at the time of the experience, I did not interpret it in a way that is open to easy ridicule.

At the time I lived in an inner Sydney working-class suburb.

It was the last month or so of my final year at school. I was greatly perplexed about what to do the next year. It was expected that I would go to university. But to study what? The choice seemed so big and final. You choose your degree course, spend several youthful years in hard study, graduate and then spend the rest of your life working at what the degree qualified you for.

My father was keen for me to study law. In his policeman's world, it was barristers who made all the money. His heart was set on his only son going to the bar. For some reason— impossible for me now to comprehend how I entertained the idea— I thought I might take up dentistry. But in a way peculiar to our youth, I was deeply confused and in total angst about making such a seemingly fateful choice.

Because I had recently 'got religion', someone— and I cannot remember who it was— suggested I might be a priest. My reply was, 'Oh, yeah, likely!' Clergy had had no influence on my life and I thought the few I had met, mostly via religious lessons at school, were odd and, to use a term permissible in those days, 'unmanly'.

My family's house had only an outside loo. Customarily, my daily session was after dinner at night. I never turned on the light, but left the door open. Darkness kept me from view.

For me, loo time was thinking time. In those days, I had never heard that Martin Luther was 'on the privy in the tower' when he had his theological revelation of the true nature of grace which sparked off the European Reformation and helped shape the modern world. My thoughts were never so grandiose. But at this period of my life, loo time had become agonising thinking time. 'What was I going to do when I left school at the end of the year?'

While I was deep in these musings, an unusual event occurred. I saw a meteorite flash across the sky. I recall thinking, 'I've been sitting here most nights for years and that's the first time I've ever seen a meteorite.' I told my parents of the sighting, but thought nothing more of it. Until the next night.

There I was again. Same time, same after-dinner loo session, same door open. And the same agonising thoughts about what to study at university the next year. That was all usual.

What was unusual was a second sighting of a meteorite. I thought, 'Years and years and never a one, now a meteorite two nights running'. I confess I did ask myself if this was some sort of sign, whether there was any meaning to it. The brushed-off suggestion about the priesthood did come to my mind.

In those days, my father said he was an atheist, so I had never mentioned the suggestion about priesthood as a vocation to either of my parents. I had not taken it seriously anyway. This time I did not tell them about the meteorite sighting either.

On the following night, I saw a third meteorite in the same circumstances. Internally, I became convinced that I should explore the possibility of a calling to the ministry of the church. Initially, my application to commence studies was refused. I was considered too young. After some prescribed work experience and university studies, I was accepted, at age nineteen, thirty-four years ago as I write.

For a few weeks— and take into account I was only seventeen at the time— I entertained the idea that God had intentionally 'flicked' those meteorites across the sky for me. A miracle! It is a story capable of such dramatic interpretation.

I soon learnt from an astronomy text that it was the usual time of the year for meteorite showers. I accepted that the meteorites were not 'sent' for me. But the conviction that this was, nevertheless, a theophany (a word I had not heard of then) remained. I continued to accept that the totality of the experience constituted my 'call' to serve God in the ministry of the church.

I quickly stopped telling the story of what happened because I had no way of making it sound sensible to anyone else. It was many years before I understood the dual nature of what we call the 'out there' world which I have since come to understand as always a combination of what is actually 'there' and our 'in here' perceptions of it. It was years later, too, before I discovered Dostoevsky's notion of 'coincidences', Carl Jung's 'synchronicity' or the whole world of intuitive and mystical intelligence.

Even after these discoveries, I kept the experience in the closet until now. Its interpretation will have to wait until the next chapter because I want to examine more actual stories of people's theophanies.

✠ Theophanies in the Bible

There are many such stories in the Bible. Most are theophanies of the ordinary kind, such as Merton's inner voice, and they tend to be introduced by stock phrases like, 'And the word of the Lord came to me saying . . .'. That is to say, someone— often termed a seer, prophet or apostle — has sensed that God has spoken to them in a mystical experience. Shortly, I will look at this sort of theophany with another example from my own experience.

Much more unusually, the Bible tells stories about dramatic and visionary theophanies. Most famous of these, known to just about anyone with an acquaintance with the English language, is the conversion of St Paul on the road to Damascus. English speakers know of it, even if they have never actually heard the biblical story, because a 'Damascus Road conversion' has become idiomatic English for any dramatic change of mind or direction by anyone, especially in political circles. Unless the Bible's accounts of such visionary theophanies are read with a good sense of its literary styles, conventions, symbols and levels, most of these stories will seem quite stupid.

There are four versions of St Paul's conversion theophany in the Bible. Three are in the Acts of the Apostles and one, by Paul himself, is in his Letter to the Galatians. It is the dramatic stories in Acts that are well known.

Paul's own version in what was originally just a letter is simple and prosaic. The bare facts are the same as in the stories in Acts. He speaks of his Jewish religious education and zeal, his persecution of what he saw as Jesus' heretical Jewish sect and his change of mind in seeing Jesus instead as God's agent—which included sensing his own destiny to take the religion of Jesus the Jew to non-Jews (Gentiles). His own account is as follows:

> For I want you to know, brothers and sisters, that the gospel that was proclaimed by me is not of human origin; for I did not receive it from a human source, nor was I taught it, but I received it through a revelation of Jesus Christ.
>
> You have heard no doubt of my earlier life in Judaism. I was violently persecuting the church of God and was trying to destroy it. I advanced in Judaism beyond many among my people of the same age, for I was far more zealous for the tradition of my ancestors. But when God, who had set me apart before I was born and called me through his grace, was pleased to reveal his Son to me, so that I might proclaim him among the Gentiles, I did not confer with any human being.[10]

This account of Paul's theophany was written some decades before the stories in Acts. With restraint of style, Paul speaks clearly of a theophany in which he came to reverse his opinion about Jesus as the Jewish Messiah (the Christ). His experience is mystical: 'I received it through a revelation,' he says. 'God . . . was pleased to reveal his Son to me.' But there are none of the 'bells, whistles and flashing lights' of the dramatic and visionary style of the story as told in the Acts of the Apostles.

The three versions told in Acts are not internally consistent. We have no way of telling whether the unknown author (by tradition, St Luke) had access to any account by Paul himself of the outer circumstances of his theophany. It could be that the writer of Acts has taken Paul's own account of his theophany and written it in the style of a literary drama.

Creating God as a character among characters is a common literary device in the Bible and is not generally seen as God literally speaking. (Moses and the Burning Bush is an excellent example of a theophany story where God is behind 'God the character'.) It is notoriously difficult to put into everyday language a mystical experience which transcends but intersects with the everyday world. Dramatic storytelling is helpful so long as it is not taken literally. Literal interpretation turns God's mystical relationship with the world into a magical one.

The following account from the Acts of the Apostles of St Paul's Damascus Road experience reads quite differently from his own story. It uses his Hebrew name, Saul, rather than his Roman name, 'Paul':

Meanwhile Saul, still breathing threats and murder against the disciples of the Lord, went to the High Priest and asked

him for letters to the synagogues at Damascus, so that if he
found any that belonged to the Way, men or women, he
might bring them bound to Jerusalem.

Now as he was going along and approaching Damascus,
suddenly a light from heaven flashed around him. He fell to
the ground and heard a voice saying to him, 'Saul, Saul, why
do you persecute me?' He asked, 'Who are you, Lord?' The
reply came, 'I am Jesus whom you are persecuting. But get
up and enter the city, and you will be told what you are to
do.'

The men who were travelling with him stood speechless,
because they heard the voice but saw no one. Saul got up
from the ground and, though his eyes were open, he could
see nothing; so they led him by the hand and brought him
into Damascus. For three days, he was without sight, and
neither ate nor drank.[11]

✠ Leo Tolstoy's 'in the pits' theophany

Not infrequently, people experience a theophany when they are
in the pits, even so deep in the pits that they are suicidal. Perhaps
this is because depression expands the focus of consciousness,
opening it to possibilities of experience ordinarily excluded.
Perhaps it is because God's love is more insistent upon us in
our need and sorrow. This will be explored in a later chapter.

An example of an 'in the pits' theophany is the story of the
Russian author, Leo Tolstoy:

I remember one day in early spring, I was alone in the forest,
lending my ear to its mysterious noises. I listened, and my
thought went back to what for these three years it was always
busy with—the quest of God. But the idea of him, I said,
how did I ever come by the idea?

And again there arose in me, with this thought, glad

aspirations towards life. Everything in me awoke and received a meaning . . .

Why do I look further? a voice within me asked. He is there: he, without whom one cannot live. To acknowledge God and to live are one and the same thing. God is what life is. Well, then! live, seek God, and there will be no life without him . . .

After this, things cleared up within me and about me better than ever, and the light has never wholly died away. I was saved from suicide. Just how or when the change took place I cannot tell. But as insensibly and gradually as the force of life had been annulled within me and I had reached my moral death-bed, just as gradually and imperceptibly did the energy of life come back.[12]

✠ Interpreting theophanies

As I have said, it is easy to talk about the circumstances in which a theophany is experienced—a slip in the mud, the sight of a meteorite, the sounds of a forest. But it is exceedingly difficult to communicate the actual experience. The words and images of everyday life never adequately conjure up the 'otherness' of what has happened. Frequent resort is made to such terms as 'vision', 'light', 'inner voice'. Tolstoy speaks of 'a voice within me'.

As we noted earlier, most biblical theophany is ordinary, not dramatic and visionary. The report of it is introduced by such phrases as, 'Thus said the Lord to me' or 'The word of the Lord came unto me saying'. The naive might accept (or reject) this kind of talk literally and aurally, ignoring the mystical process behind it. This is not to deny that there are, and always have been, those who prattle about 'The Lord said to me'—reflecting not a legitimate mystical experience, but only their own mental processes.

✠ Interpreting a theophany of my own

In 1980, I experienced a theophany which, if I chose, could be reported simply as:

> The word of the Lord came to me saying, 'You shall concentrate on me alone'.

In one sense, this is entirely accurate; in another sense, it is entirely misleading.

In 1979, I set aside work on my doctoral studies because I felt they were not assisting my search for truth and personal growth. They were too narrow in scope. I could see no purpose for continuing, other than the title at the end. Instead, I decided to write a book. This was published in 1980 with the title, *The Human Journey: Christianity and Modern Consciousness.*

As for most authors, that first book is now something of an embarrassment. At the time, it sought to synthesise various life experiences with my studies in literature, theology, history, psychology and sociology. Within the limits imposed by its intended readership, it was a book of reason and rational argument. Not long after completing it, I fell into a severe depression.

I suffered from mild depression from the ages of thirteen to twenty-nine. It was not clinical depression. I never sought or received any medical treatment or counselling for it. It was a very private experience, shared only with intimate friends. I knew its source was my relationship with my mother, who did suffer from clinical depression. This is why I am probably so fond of saying, even today, that we never grow up until we sort out our relationship with Mum and Dad. (We can never deal with God, incidentally, until we have done that, too; otherwise Mum, Dad and God get very confused. This is as true of atheists and agnostics as it is of believers.)

By the time I was twenty-nine, I had pretty well sorted out my relationship with my mother and my depression disappeared. It returned when I was thirty-eight, just after I had come back from London and the UK launch of *The Human Journey*.

This depression was deeper than those of my earlier life. I knew this one had nothing to do with my relationship with my mother. I could not discern any cause for it which, perhaps, is why it was worse than any previous depression.

I was rector of an Anglican church in Paddington, in inner-city Sydney. Outwardly, I was able to carry on with all my work responsibilities. My parishioners had no idea of my dark internal state. Inwardly, I survived by spending several hours each day lying on the carpet in front of the altar in the quietness of my locked church. I had no idea why I was doing this. It just seemed appropriate.

As I lay in front of the altar, I did not sleep or pray intentionally with words. I was just *there*. Mostly, my mind free-flowed in uncontrolled silent words and images, a kind of wide-awake dream. Sometimes, the flow would cease and I would simply 'be'— in content-less consciousness. As the weeks passed, I began to feel better, especially after the experiences of 'being-without-content'. I began to seek this state intentionally. I should say, too, that at this time I had never heard of what is called 'relaxation therapy', nor do I equate my experience with that particular remedial technique.

St George's Church in Paddington has two large domed lights hanging just above head height from its high gothic ceiling. I would gaze at one of these lights, intentionally seeking to be conscious of nothing else. It took effort— not the effort of focus and concentration, but of letting go, a relaxation of body and mind. Eventually, I taught myself to achieve this state quite quickly. But something very odd and surprising started to occur. I would become aware not of myself looking at the light, but of myself looking at myself looking at the light. Two 'myselfs'. It was as if one 'myself' and the light existed in the same world together, whilst the other 'myself' looked on from somewhere else.

I told no-one of this experience. My wife first heard about it when she read this chapter in draft form. It seemed too weird to tell. But with this new and intentional practice, two things happened rapidly:

- the cloud of my deep depression became lighter and lighter;
- I became super-aware of the world around me, as if it were all shining, fresh and wonderful.

One day in this state of looking at myself looking at the light, there was an inner voice. Yet it is silly to say 'voice'. I heard no sound and there were no actual words. But the 'voice' said, 'You shall concentrate on me alone'. At least, that is the only way I can communicate what it said. And in one sense, it is an entirely accurate expression of the 'message'.

After this, I ceased my daily sessions lying in front of the altar. They had lasted over five months. The need had gone. My depression disappeared. I returned to my normal work. Most significantly, with two close friends I founded the Eremos Institute.

Eremos is Greek for desert. 'To promote Christian spirituality in the Australian context' was the purpose of Eremos. It was to become, with some success, a balance between the rationalistic culture of the modern church and secular society. We did not intend Eremos to be anti-reason but mystical, going beyond the limits of the rational. There are obvious connections between my 'you-shall-concentrate-on-me-alone' theophany and the founding of Eremos. As with those embarrassing meteorites, I will return to this theophany in the next chapter.

Most theophanies, including most of mine, are very ordinary. God breaks through to us from spring blossoms on a cherry tree, the dance of autumn leaves in a breeze, the eyes of a child, the weathered lines on an elderly face, a summer's night, the diorama of a winter fire, the crashing of thunder in a storm, the loving voice of a friend, the restless tossings of insomnia. Theophanies are our signposts. They invite us to the reality behind reality— to travel life as a journey, a journey towards home.

On our part, all that is needed is attentiveness. If we fail to pay attention to our theophanies, the intended journey home turns into a mere treading of ever-narrowing circles.

2.

Foolery

Seeing differently in order to see

For you know, nuncle,
The hedge-sparrow fed the cuckoo so long
That it had its head bit off by its young.
So out went the candle, and we were left darkling.

So SAYS THE FOOL IN ACT 1, SCENE 4 OF SHAKESPEARE'S play *King Lear*. In old age, Lear in his vanity wishes to retain the status and dignity of a king, but to hand over the actual task of ruling to his three daughters. Effectively, he holds an auction to divide the kingdom between them, an auction in which flattery is the coin of exchange.

In their greed for gain and power, his daughters Goneril and Regan play along with Lear's game and pay up with the flattery his vanity desires. Cordelia, who truly loves her father and is his favourite, refuses to indulge her father's foolish fantasy. Rashly, Lear immediately casts her off. This, we are told, is not just a fault of his old age, for he 'hath ever but slenderly known himself'.

Goneril and Regan prove utterly faithless, taking their father's power to rule and paying him none of his desired respect. Lear's kingdom becomes the rule of wrong, not right, where the king is a fool and the king's fool wise. Lear is the hedge-sparrow whose head Goneril and Regan will bite off.

In Shakespeare, it is often the Fool who speaks the most wise truth. All the 'normals' live in a world of self-deceit and illusion which they do not see until they are literally undone. For them, the Fool is a source of witty, frequently bawdy entertainment. On the odd occasions when the Fool's wisdom gets through to the self-deluded, he is turned on with anger or even violence.

✠ Theophany and culture

Though by saying this I chance being the true, not wise, fool of the one soldier in step, it seems to me that secular Western culture, by virtue of its secularity, is a world of public illusion and self-deceit passing for sanity, but heading for tragedy. Religion is its fool— or should be.

It was 'foolish' to tell the story of my youthful meteorite theophany. Such a story has no place at all in secular sanity— at least, not public secular sanity. Those who hide their spirituality in the closet, who know, as it were, that there is 'a ghost in the machine'— and I suspect it is all of us— will at best be cautiously open. But not in public. 'It hardly does', as Patrick White said, to go around speaking of such things publicly. Normal people living in a normal world are not expected to have theophanies, not even with God in private. Theophanies are not part of reality. But whose reality?

This was precisely the question I was left with by my 'St George's light' theophany. *Whose* reality?

I was supposed to be a spiritual leader, but where was the Spirit? I had allowed myself to be trapped into just one way of experiencing reality: the way of secular intellectual reason.

Writing a whole book based solely on intellectual reason left me emotionally exhausted. Worse, it exposed me as spiritually barren.

The experience of looking at myself looking at the light reawakened my mystical perception. It did not negate the value of intellectual reason; it simply exposed its limitations, especially in its secular form.

William Blake's words rang with fresh truth:

If the doors of perception were cleansed,
everything would appear to man as it is,
infinite.
For man has closed himself up, till he
sees things thro' chinks of his cavern.

I understand Blake to mean that there are different ways of knowing and that for human beings to be whole and integrated they must draw on them all. We must not narrow our vision with blinkers. This is what I understood 'You must concentrate on me alone' to mean. I interpreted it as saying, 'You haven't been experiencing God and life at all—just intellectualising.'

✠ Theophany as a way of knowing

In matters spiritual, I am a slow learner. This was a lesson I could have taken to heart some fifteen years earlier, at the end of my undergraduate theological studies.

I studied and trained for the Anglican ministry at Moore Theological College in Sydney and through London University. My training at Moore College was rigorously rational. We learnt Greek, some Hebrew, systematic theology, church history, philosophical theology, ethics, pastoral care, and intellectually demanding methods of interpreting the text of the Bible. From fairly close acquaintance, I believe the core of such training was and is typical of ordination training in any Western theological college or seminary, be it Anglican, Catholic or Protestant.

It is assumed, validly in most cases, that a student will arrive at a college or seminary with a felt, experiential, theophanic sense of God. Also it is assumed that, as well as providing some actual skills of spiritual ministry, the core purpose of training is to provide a reasoned basis for the felt, theophanic experience of God.

The contents of the actual reasoning will vary from spiritual tradition to spiritual tradition: Calvin's or Moltmann's, say, in a Protestant college, Aquinas' or Rahner's in a Catholic seminary. But intellectual reason remains central in every case. When the studies touch on the modern secular world, the issues here, too, are those of intellectual reason. They include such questions as:

- Is the Bible reliable?
- What is true in the stories about Jesus?
- Does God exist?
- What is the origin of evil?
- Are miracles possible?

By the third of my four years of this kind of study, I was so confused that I decided to become an atheist. Only my most intimate friends were told. It was not a confusion about the content of my studies. I understood the content quite well and was awarded my Licentiate that same year with honours. What was confusing was the lack of connection between the systematic, abstract reasoning and my theophanic, mystical experience of God.

What was even more confusing was the tension between the certitude of those mystical experiences and the stalemate of either blind doubt or blind faith at the end of every rational process. By this method, you could never know whether God existed or whether God did not exist. You could not prove that Jesus rose from the dead or disprove it either.

We learnt from Joseph Butler, the esteemed philosopher– bishop of the eighteenth century, that all proof, whether in science or religion, is a matter of statistical probability, not certainty. But in science, where you can measure and count, statistical probabilities make sense.

'How wide or heavy is God?' I recall thinking. It seemed absurd that statistical probabilities could be applied to the existence of God, to the divinity or humanity of Christ, or to the historical reliability of the Bible. There was nothing to count except reasoned arguments, which always seemed to cancel one another out.

My atheism did not last the year out. I found it unbelievable. A point of certitude again at last!

At the end of my fourth year in December 1965, aged twenty-three, I was ordained by Archbishop Hugh Gough at St Andrew's Cathedral in Sydney. I didn't believe anything much, but I still 'knew'. Only this knowing gave me the personal integrity to proceed with my ordination.

How, why or with what detail I knew I could not have articulated. I presumed my colleagues proceeded with their ordi- nation— there were more than twenty of us— because they knew and also had reasons. I doubted the validity of the reasons I presumed them to have, but my gut said 'knowing' was more important anyway.

✠ University pursuits in the light of my theophanies

With little trust in intellectual theology, I searched for reasons elsewhere. In turn, I studied seriously at university history, literature and sociology. I also read widely in science and philosophy. A wariness of the kind of chronological snobbery which holds that new and latest is best kept me cautious about abandoning mainstream Christianity.

Thus, I did not fall for the faddism of the 'God-is-Dead' and so-called 'secular' theologies of the over-confident late 1960s and early 1970s. By 1978, I felt I had found enough 'reasons' and sought to popularise them by writing *The Human Journey*. You know the hole I then fell into.

Hindsight is an exact science. Through the 'St George's light' theophany, I realised I had travelled down the exact same intellectual-reason road into which I had been inducted. Not only my study of theology, but also my study of history, sociology, science, philosophy and, to a large extent, literature led me down this same road. *The Human Journey* was just my 'popularised' version of it.

I need to say that although it somewhat embarrasses me now, I do not reject what I said in that book. I simply see it as one-tracked and limited. Nor do I reject intellectual reason. But I do see it as a *restricted* way of knowing—in the end a spiritual wasteland.

✠ Patrick White's intuitive 'knowing'

Patrick White said that, increasingly, he hoped his novels might 'give professed unbelievers glimpses of their own unprofessed faith'. He believed that 'out there' was a reading public whose religion was in the closet because they 'are afraid that by admitting it they will forfeit their right to be considered intellectuals'. He also confessed (in a private letter) that it was easier for him to admit his spirituality 'because I am not an intellectual'.[1]

White is both serious and very tongue-in-cheek when he says 'I am not an intellectual'— serious because he saw himself as an intuitive and because he valued intuitive knowing above the rational knowing of intellectuals. He described a Catholic nun who visited him while doing research for a postgraduate thesis on his writings as 'extremely intelligent . . . far more intellectual than I'. But he complained that:

> She was trying desperately hard to keep things on a rational plane, whereas I was bringing it back all the time to an intuitive one.[2]

White is ironically tongue-in-cheek about not being an intellectual because his own wide reading, prodigious memory and powers of rational intelligence were more than enough to qualify him for life membership of that club. But he did not wish to join a club whose membership required perceptual blinkers.

Seeing myself seeing myself looking at the light in St George's church removed my rational intelligence blinkers. I became aware again that consciousness is much more than what D.H. Lawrence scathingly termed 'mere head knowledge'. I had this awareness at the time of my ordination. I was ordained because 'I knew': knew in the sense of Patrick White's intuitive knowing. But I did not know how to follow up this insight. Neither church nor university was much help. Both in their own way sought acceptance and respectability by conforming to the rational intelligence club. I could find no wise fool.

✠ Learning to be mystical and intuitive

I left St George's Paddington at the end of 1983. My new appointment was in Canberra as head of the Anglican Church's theological college in that city. Within a few months, I was also appointed assistant bishop of the diocese based in Canberra. At college, my teaching responsibilities were Systematic Theology and Sociology of Religion.

I was determined that my students learn more about self and consciousness than can be gleaned by rational intelligence. I was just as determined that they achieve excellence in that way of knowing, too. I gained a reputation, I think, for being rigorous about the latter and puzzling about the former. 'Puzzling' is probably too soft and polite a word for the reaction of some of my students to my attempts to inculcate in them an intuitive and mystical consciousness.

From my side, the side of teacher and lecturer, the problem was that the students were already thoroughly socialised into the mindset of what White calls the 'intellectuals'. Most, but not all, were university graduates. Except for one, all had grown up and gone to school in a secular, Westernised culture— most in Australia. Thus, graduate and non-graduate alike took for granted that knowing was rational knowing.

Every one of them had had some kind of theophanic experience. It was this that brought them to the college in the first place. Yet the expectation was that, somehow, rational intelligence would both supply supporting reasons for this experience and build on it. There was no notion that their experience might call into question the limitations of rational intelligence and require them to explore other ways of knowing and understanding.

T.S. Eliot complains about people who speak of 'vague emotion' and 'clear thought'. He held strongly to the conviction that thought is more often vague and emotion precise. Rightly or wrongly, I felt most of my students, through no fault of their own (the fault lay in their secular, rational education), were light years from such an understanding. If I had said, 'Words speak to the mind and music to the soul', the musical among them would have understood. But even they, I guessed, would not see music as an equally valid way of knowing truth as intellectual reason.

It was with a perception of these obstacles and difficulties that I set out to try to expand my students' sense of consciousness and knowing. In hindsight, I may have been more successful by entering the lecture room and remaining silent for fifty minutes (this is the way of George Fox's Quakers), or to have set them the puzzle of a Zen Koan, even the well-known 'Listen for the sound of one hand clapping' (Koans are designed to expand tunnel vision). But realising we usually learn by moving step-by-step from what we do know to what we don't know, I took the safer course of trying to build a bridge between rational knowing and other ways of knowing. Reason and emotion seemed a good place to start.

I would ask the students, 'What is the difference between emotional reason and rational reason?' Most students found the question very odd. Like me, they had grown up in a culture in which they had learnt to see reason and emotion as opposites. By definition emotion lacked, and was an antonym for, reason. To speak of emotional reason seemed contradictory and absurd, an oxymoron of the first order.

In the case of rational reason, the criterion of discernment is logicality. Thus, in the simplistic world of the classroom, it is easy to demonstrate the illogicality of the following statement:

Either it is raining or it is not raining.
It is not raining.
Therefore, it is raining.

The opening statement contains mutually exclusive conditions: it rains or it does not rain. Therefore, we reject the 'deductive' conclusion as illogical and invalid.

None of the students had any difficulty with this. They were schooled from an early age in the discernment of rational reason. Some, especially those who had had legal training, were much better at it than I.

Emotional reason, though, was another matter altogether. The general view was that, in essence, emotions were unreliable, they carried you away, you could not trust them. An alternative view allowed trust in emotions, but viewed them as entirely subjective. You like something because it feels good or right for you. That is it. There is nothing further to talk about; no conversation is possible. There is no criterion of emotional discernment except subjective 'like' or 'dislike'. Feelings have no reason to them.

It is not my intention to criticise my students for this way of seeing things. They were, to a man and woman, fine people who taught me much more than ever I taught them. Their view of emotions as either unreliable or totally subjective was part of their heritage in modern, secular, Western culture—part of the sanity!

But to try to widen their Westernised tunnel vision, I would ask:

Is there a qualitative, evaluative difference between, say, the emotion experienced by a drunk pleasurably smashing bottles in a gutter and, say, the emotion experienced by a person pleasurably listening to a Mozart symphony?

Invariably, the answer was 'yes'. No-one, interestingly, ever ventured the purely subjectivist view 'to each her own—there's no difference'. The obvious difficulty was to explain what and why. Clearly, the logical–illogical categories of rational reason were not going to assist. At this point, I would introduce the words 'sensibility' and 'sentimentality', saying:

> As categories of discernment, what logicality and illogicality
> are to rational reason, so are sensibility and sentimentality to
> emotional reason.

If puzzlement remained in student minds, we would talk about such simple distinctions as the difference between teenage puppy love (sentimentality) and adult married love (sensibility). This also helped to demonstrate that emotional reason applied to everyday life, not just to the 'higher', 'refined' feelings of music and the other arts.

Pascal said, 'The heart has reasons that the mind knows not of'. This is a truth more dead than alive in modern, secular culture. But the heart has unreason, too: misleading, untruthful, destructive, sentimental emotions. Often those with the most sharply honed rational reason fall prey to sentimental, emotional unreason.

I think of Jean Paul Sartre, the French philosopher, as an example. Even in old age, his erotic emotions remained fixated on young girls, with no capacity to relate to his whole being. His partner, Simone de Beauvoir, remained his intellectual, artistic and political companion. That she put up with Sartre's near-bimbo liaisons suggests that she, too, another rationalistic philosopher, was sentimental about her love (obsession?) for Sartre.

For the arts, emotional reason is more important than rational reason. For religion, it is the same. This is why Patrick

White saw art and intuitive knowing as the way to offer intellec-
tualised 'professed unbelievers glimpses of their own unprofessed
faith'.

Just as there is rubbishy and sentimental art, there is rubbishy
and sentimental religion. Acquiring the ability to discern the
difference demands as much rigour as learning to reason logically.
There is nothing elitist about this. Popular art and popular
religion, as well as the more sophisticated versions of both, can
express sensibility or sentimentality.

Down the centuries, the religion of Jesus has been carried as
much by its hymns and songs as by its theology. All in all, these
hymns and songs are a great treasure trove of spiritual art, of fine
poetry and music. Unfortunately for those of us living in the
twentieth century, the Victorian era spawned a huge volume of
sentimental hymns and songs which the church was slow to
jettison. Examining the flaws in this spiritual art was one way I
sought to demonstrate to my students the difference between
emotional reason and emotional unreason.

A Victorian hymn, first published in 1887 and still not
jettisoned from many current collections, was my favourite
example. It usually took a whole lecture to examine it, so, by
way of illustration, I will cite only its first line, the second verse
and the chorus which is repeated after each verse. It goes:

When we walk with the Lord . . .
Not a shadow can rise,
not a cloud in the skies,
but his smile quickly drives it away;
not a doubt or a fear,
not a sigh or a tear
can abide while we trust and obey.

> Trust and obey, for there's no other way,
> to be happy in Jesus,
> but to trust and obey.

Fine poetry is the artistic fusion of sense and sensibility; this hymn has neither. Unless already sentimentally predisposed to accept its central assertion, we must reject the idea that the common trials and troubles of humanity shall not assail those who walk with the Lord in trust and obedience. They may be comforted and strengthened in their trials and troubles, but 2000 years of Christian experience demonstrates they are not free from them. The Jesus in whom the hymn bids us to be 'happy' told his followers to take up the cross daily and follow him. This suggests that Christian discipleship is a hard, at times life-threatening, occupation, not a push-over. Such a command hardly fits with a definition of happiness as 'free from all trouble'.

As a poem, the hymn does not create; it asserts. When it does try to create, it fails. For example, shadows do not rise; they fall or are cast. (Presumably, 'rise' is chosen because it rhymes with 'skies' in the following line.) A divine smile, which the hymn asserts can drive away our sighs and sorrows, carries about as much conviction as a snake-oil salesman peddling the universal elixir. And the 'smiling' God who keeps all ills from good boys and girls simply reflects the fear of the Victorian child in the face of his/her male parent. The music to which this syrupy sentiment is set has a *thumpity thump-thump* rhythm with the same sort of subtlety of sense and sensibility as the words themselves.

As part of their ministry training, daily services of worship at college were arranged by the students themselves. From time to time, they took great delight in choosing 'Trust and obey' as the opening hymn.

✣ Is the drug-induced state another form of 'knowing'?

If emotion as well as reason is a way of knowing, what other ways are there? This question raises the issue of the nature of consciousness itself.

In the last of his six-book 'Outsider' series, Colin Wilson says:

> Man lives at the bottom of a kind of fish-tank whose glass is greasy, dusty and inclined to distort. Certain experiences can endow him with a mental energy that momentarily rockets him clear at the top of the fish-tank and he sees reality as infinitely alien, infinitely strange. What is more, it is curiously meaningful; if a direct relation could be established with it, life would be seen in the light of purpose.[3]

Wilson says it is not our five physical senses that constitute the distorting glass. What distorts are the social relationships that influence us to see in a particular way. In Shakespeare's *King Lear*, greasy fish-tank vision is the sanity of most of the main characters, a sanity they reinforce upon each other. It is the Fool who rockets to the top and sees more clearly.

Wilson wrote about 'fish-tank vision' after reporting his experiences under the influence of mescalin. Mescalin is the drug Aldous Huxley and Sartre also experimented with. Mescalin made Huxley feel, in his own words, like 'Adam at the dawn of creation'. Strange words, as Wilson notes, for a man who usually rendered the world bloodless by excessive conceptualising— a man for whom rational intelligence had become the only way of knowing.

Experimenting with mind-altering drugs is the way many Westerners, intellectual and non-intellectual, have come to see the limitations of 'normal' consciousness. In some ways, most notable is the experience of the psychologist William James, because he was such a cautious, scientific rationalist.

James experimented with nitrous oxide (laughing gas). Afterwards, he said:

> Nitrous oxide and ether, especially nitrous oxide, when sufficiently diluted with air, stimulate the mystical consciousness to an extraordinary degree. Depth beyond depth of truth seems revealed to the inhaler. This truth fades out, however, or escapes at the moment of coming to.
>
> . . . Some years ago, I myself made some observations on this aspect of nitrous oxide intoxication and reported them in print. One conclusion was forced upon my mind at that time and my impression of its truth has ever since remained unshaken. It is that our normal waking consciousness— 'rational consciousness' as we call it— is but one special type of consciousness, whilst all about it, parted from it by the filmiest of screens, there lie potential forms of consciousness entirely different . . .
>
> No account of the universe in its totality can I find which leaves these other forms of consciousness quite disregarded. How to regard them is the question— for they are so discontinuous with ordinary consciousness . . .
>
> Looking back on my own experiences, they all converge towards a kind of insight to which I cannot help ascribing some metaphysical significance. The key of it is invariably a reconciliation. It is as if the opposites of the world, whose contradictoriness and conflict make all our difficulties and troubles, were melted into unity.[4]

Three things stand out in what James says. Wilson, Huxley and others report them, too, in different words.

- Ordinary, rational consciousness only touches the surface reality of self and world.
- Drug-altered states of consciousness are (radically) discontinuous with ordinary, everyday (normal?) consciousness.
- Drug-expanded consciousness evokes a profound sense of meaning, purpose and coherence about self and world.

It is to anticipate my next chapter, but here I think it important to say that it is the artificiality of the drug-inducement of these states of consciousness that causes their discontinuity with ordinary, everyday consciousness. When expansion of consciousness is experienced as the result of intentions arising from within the self, through prayer, meditation, silence, contemplation or worship, no such discontinuity arises. My self-invented 'looking at the St George's light' meditation is an example.

Apart from those prescribed medically, alcohol and nicotine are the only drugs I have taken intentionally. One cold winter's night, I got slightly 'stoned' at a university Sociological Society party. That was the consequence of inhaling the exhaled marijuana smoke of others in a shuttered room!

Not until I was a theology undergraduate and first read William James' account of his nitrous oxide experience did I recall a similar experience of my own.

I was about eight years old at the time and had a number of teeth extracted whilst anaesthetised with laughing gas. While I was out to it, I had what I then called a dream— a more vivid dream than any experienced before or since. For no apparent reason, I was running through and admiring huge, beautiful churches. Church after church after church, as I ran and ran and ran. Most were gothic in style.

Looking back, I would call them cathedrals, but I am fairly sure I did not know that word or concept as an eight-year-old. I was not frightened, but fascinated by their haunting height and majestic depth. I saw intricate stone carvings and vast masses of coloured glass windows. The number of them seemed endless as I exited one only to enter another. I recall the enthusiasm with which I related this weird dream to my parents and their words to the effect that 'It was just the laughing gas'.

As I have said, I did not grow up in a religious family. Perhaps I had seen pictures of such churches in magazines and books. But we were not a reading family either and I cannot recall seeing such pictures. Only in my thirties, when I first visited Great Britain and Europe, did I see in 'reality' what I saw in that laughing-gas dream. It was then I began to wonder about why becoming a dentist had ever entered my head—a thought, as you will recall, that was in my mind at the time I felt a call to the priesthood.

Just how thin, I wonder, is the screen between normal, waking consciousness and that 'depth beyond depth' James writes about? I think most people experience its flimsiness sometimes, even if it is only in those moments when passing from wakefulness to sleep or when recovering from illness.

✠ The compartmentalised contradictions of Western 'sanity'

Sanity in Western culture today is a bundle of compartmentalised contradictions. In one compartment is the world of everyday life, a world of work, leisure, family and friends. The typical attitude is to live in it blind, so to speak, as if it contained its own meaning and will go on forever.

In another compartment is the dominant public orthodoxy: the so-called scientific world view. It tries to reduce everything to quantities and measures, even the human psyche. At the cosmo-mythical level, it tells us that we humans are biological accidents, the chance effluxions of a vast, impersonal, matter–energy process: meaningless ants crawling over a tenth-rate planet orbiting a third-rate star.

And in yet another compartment is our closet religion. All the sociological evidence shows that, though only a minority attend the churches of the West's traditional religion, the vast majority believe in God, pray from time to time and think of themselves as spiritual beings.

If today's secular Western culture were a Shakespearean tragedy, one might guess we are at about Act 3, with the seeds of tragic disintegration already sown. Lear's Fool might well be warning of a coming 'cold night which will turn us all to fools and madmen'.

Rational intelligence is very successful for understanding and manipulating what we call the 'external world'. The quantitative or 'hard' sciences are its crowning glory. But by putting their way of knowing, and what they know, on such a high pedestal of social approval, they render themselves meaningless and morally bereft.

There are some hopeful signs within science itself of a return to a more integrated self than our current compartmentalising. In micro-physics, for example, with Heinsenberg's uncertainty principle, the distinction between the 'out there' (observed) and the 'in here' (observer's) world has broken down. At this level, human consciousness and the 'out there' world are seen to be interactive— one influences the other.

Quite a number of physicists and leading scientists in other fields have begun to speak of God and a meaningful universe again. But they are still using only one tool of knowing: rational intelligence. And still coming up with the same old 'you can't prove but you can't disprove' conclusions.

In states of consciousness different from ordinary, rational consciousness, albeit drug-induced, people such as James and Huxley experienced a profound sense of meaning and purpose about both self and universe. The application of rational intelligence to the 'external world' has produced the opposite. We become meaningless ants. But science, until forced to do so in modern micro-physics, has all but ignored consciousness itself.

Looking at myself looking at the light in St George's church awakened me to the spiritual barrenness of reducing knowing to the intellect. A few months after this experience, I read Colin Wilson's last 'Outsider' series book. Drawing on Whitehead and Husserl, whom I had not then read, what Wilson said helped make sense of my own weird experience and what was happening to secular Western culture:

> Man owes his evolutionary primacy to his faculty of immediacy perception, concentrating a narrow beam of attention on the present. Animals possess so little of this power that it might be said they exist in only one mode of perception.
>
> Man possesses not only immediacy perception; he also possesses the power of conceptual analysis and imagination. Inevitably, then, he exists on several levels and, since immediacy perception demands first place, he is chiefly aware of himself as a passive consciousness . . . the more man develops this faculty of selecting and excluding, the further he retreats from meaning-perception. This is to say that the more highly

developed the intellect, and the faculty for focussing attention, the more the world is seen as meaningless.[5]

In other words, the more we rely only on rational knowing of the 'external world', the more everything appears to be meaningless. Not that everything is meaningless, but it appears meaningless because of the way we self-limit consciousness. Our wisdom becomes foolishness. Our socially defined sanity becomes a world where, as Patrick White says, it doesn't do to publicly confess that your art is inspired by God.

What we need are other ways of knowing, an expanded view of consciousness itself and of the possibilities of what may be experienced rather than just talked about.

Suppose, for the sake of argument, that the interminable rational intelligence debate, 'Does God exist?', did actually reach a water-tight conclusion and the answer was unequivocally 'Yes'. What difference would it make? It would be about as relevant as absolute logical proof that there is intelligent life on Planet 14 in Galaxy 402. Unless we could make contact with, and share in the life of, the 14/402s, such certain information about their existence would make no difference to us at all. The question of God is the same.

Colin Wilson is aware that there exists a way of knowing—mystical religion—which actually reverses the appearance of meaninglessness deriving from our over-emphasis on the intellect and the 'external world'. He says:

What is usually called 'mystical experience' is a temporary reversal of the usual order of presentational immediacy and causal efficacy, without the usual weakening of immediacy (that occurs, for example, when meaning is glimpsed on the edge of sleep). But the usual price of these 'mystical experiences' has been the inability to convey their essence in language.[6]

We observed in the last chapter the great difficulty of translating mystical, theophanic experiences into the language of the everyday world. Wilson's comment repeats this. But for all his insight, Wilson has remained a rationalist. In later books, he explores fringe spiritualities such as Extra Sensory Perception and even dowsing (water-divining), but not the mysticism of the great traditions. He continues to seek a new rationalism rather than other ways of knowing.

And he is wrong to see the effects of mystical experience as merely temporary. None of the stories of theophanic experience told in the last chapter had just a temporary effect. White, Merton, St Paul and Tolstoy all experienced self and world enduringly differently after their 'mystical experiences'.

Also, as said in the last chapter, most theophanies are ordinary and frequent. If we are attentive, we experience them nearly every day. Of course, if the aerial is down and the receiver turned off, we hear and see nothing.

The religion of Christ is the great tradition of Western culture. But in essence and origin it is an *Eastern* religion. Its heart is mystical, not rational. This, I am convinced, is the rediscovery necessary to reverse the disintegration of self and world in the West. But before going on to explore what this means, some final words about my meteorite theophany.

✠ Theophany or immature allusion?

You will recall that I had this experience when I was only seventeen. Its effect has continued ever since, as first I trained for and then entered a life as a clergyman.

Was it a boyish illusion? If I believed in a magical God who 'flicked' those meteorites across the sky just for me, then I think the answer would be 'yes' and I would be in grave doubt today about continuing as a priest and bishop. But as I said, even as a seventeen-year-old I quickly rejected that explanation. The meteorites would have streaked across the southern skies regardless of my seeing them— regardless of my nightly loo ritual; regardless of my schoolboy agonising about the future; regardless of me. Many other people must have seen those meteorites, too, and felt no call to the priesthood. I assume, also, that many people have slipped in the mud and fallen on their backs without experiencing a theophany.

Dostoevsky speaks of coincidences that cannot just be put down to chance. They are too meaningful. 'Coincidence' in such cases is a word we need to place in inverted commas. He means, for example, significant but seemingly chance meetings with another person. 'Coincidences' can also be seemingly random but pregnantly meaningful events— say, a job opening, coming across a particular film or book, or even experiencing illness or an accident.

Critical is the 'coincidental' timing of the outer and the inner experience. For example, I recall meeting on a beach far from either of our homes, amongst a crowd of sunbathers and surfers, without either of us knowing the other would be there, a woman with whom I was in love. It was a reciprocated love, but we each knew it could not continue and had parted. Our meeting was a 'coincidence'.

It was a 'coincidence', too, that my seventeen-year-old self, agonising about the future, saw, sitting on the loo, a meteorite three nights in a row. Perhaps I had never seen them before because I had not looked. Probably so. Perhaps my eyes were focussed on the sky only in that period of extreme mental tossing. Certainly, on the third night I *was* gazing purposefully for a meteorite. But not on the other two nights. The meteorites did not constitute my theophany. Theophany was the totality of the experience, inner and outer, plus the coincidental timing.

Carl Jung took the notion of coincidence further with his term 'synchronicity'. He uses this word to describe a meaningful coincidence or equivalence between a psychic and a physical state or event which have no causal relationship to one another in the usual sense.

He cites quite a number of actual examples in his autobiography, *Memories, Dreams, Reflections*. Most are exceedingly complex. The simplest is this:

> The unconscious helps by communicating things to us, or making figurative allusions. It has other ways, too, of informing us of things which by all logic we could not possibly know. Consider synchronistic phenomena, premonitions and dreams that come true.
>
> I recall one time during the Second World War when I was returning home from Bollinger. I had a book with me, but could not read, for the moment the train started to move, I was overpowered by the image of someone drowning. This was the memory of an accident that had happened while I was on military service. During the entire journey, I could not rid myself of it. It struck me as uncanny and I thought, 'What has happened? Can there have been an accident?'
>
> I got out at Erlanbach and walked home, still troubled by this memory. My second daughter's children were in

the garden. The family was living with us, having returned to Switzerland from Paris because of the war. The children stood looking upset and, when I asked, 'Why? What is the matter?', they told me that Adrian, then the youngest of the boys, had fallen into deep water in the boathouse. It is quite deep there and, since he could not really swim, he had almost drowned. His older brother had fished him out.

This had taken place at exactly the time I had been assailed by that memory in the train. The unconscious had given me a hint. Why should it not be able to inform me of other things also? [7]

Not for one moment do I think God put those meteorites in the sky just for me. God's relationship to us and the universe is mystical, not magical. But it is quite another matter to understand, as I do, God using the synchronicity of the meteorite showers and my own inner struggles to 'call' me to spiritual leadership. That everything is related to everything else is an insight not only of Jung's 'collective unconscious', but also of Einstein's 'relativity'.

What there is to be known is not limited to rational intelligence—is it?

3.

Insanity

Going mad in order to be sane

PROBABLY NOTHING MAKES ME ANGRIER THAN PEOPLE who patronise my religion as a sop—a crutch I need and they don't. I do find my religion comforting but, even more, I find it challenging.

I also get angry about people who only pray when they are in trouble or want something. They convey the impression that religion really *is* a sop! Who are they addressing with their prayers? Some conjurer? Some wizard wonder-worker? Do they think of God as a magician with a hat full of rabbits?

Now, I am not against praying when we are in trouble or even asking for things, especially if it is for our daily bread. But the essence of prayer is being known and listening, not the recitation of a wish list. Prayer is the soul's mirror. Prayer is one of life's greatest challenges, not its last resort.

Once, when chatting away with two friends, one of them asked, 'What do you *never* pray about?' The other friend replied sharply, 'My mother'. Surprised, I enquired innocently, 'Why?' 'Because I hate her,' was his bitter answer. He understood what prayer is all about! To pray is to face self-truth, not avoid it.

✠ Freud's view that religion is insanity

Sigmund Freud is most responsible for secular society's wide-spread view that religion is a sop for those who need it. Apparently, most people do still need it. But the threat of public shame drives their consumption into the private closet.

By defining religion as pathological, Freud gave birth to a new definition of sanity. No longer were religionists just illogical— they were sick. No longer was belief in God just irrational— it was neurotic. Freud believed he had scientifically discovered the origin of belief in God as an illusion.

As in the case of Karl Marx, who explained the G-O-D illusion as a social drug of the poor and oppressed, 'the opium of the people', Freud drew on the idea of projection. In simple terms, for Freud G-O-D was an illusory projection of 'Daddy' onto a cosmic screen by the psyches of those unable or afraid to grow up. God was simply Father writ large: an infantile wish fulfilment for the return of the all-powerful protector of childhood. Hence, belief in God is not only illogical, but psycho-pathological. If you want to be adult and integrated, you must jettison God— along with Santa Claus and the Tooth Fairy.

This kind of atheism appeared to be more powerful than the traditional philosophical objections to God. It had the appeal of science and explained why people entertained the idea of God in the first place.

Freud thought the psychoanalysis he invented was thoroughly scientific. He believed he was doing no less than applying the tried and proven methods of the hard sciences, such as physics or chemistry, to a new field— the psyche. He was probably sincere in this belief. I know no-one today who would agree with him. But it was a most convenient notion for a new discipline seeking acceptance in a culture where science had become the prestigious way of knowing. Freud's medical training assisted the perception of psychoanalysis as scientific.

To properly examine the flaws in Freud's belief would take a chapter itself. But briefly there are two major ones. First, the psyche is not an external object in the sense that physics and chemistry study external objects. The psyche is part of the internal subjectivity of human consciousness. It can respond to, and quite easily deceive, those who wish to study it as an object.

Second, consciousness is our faculty of knowing. Until the arrival of modern micro-physics, real scientists could get away with ignoring consciousness and just use it to get on with their research. But Freud wanted to study consciousness itself. How is this possible? It is certainly quite a different issue from the mere application of scientific method to a new field. Does the psyche observe the psyche? Or is there a more fundamental part of consciousness, say the spirit or the soul, which observes the psyche? Freud did not even raise these fundamental issues.

When I was in my early thirties, I spent a year reading just about everything Freud ever wrote. I had no illusion that I was reading science, but I gained great profit from entering a mind and soul as large as Freud's. Freud is an artist of the human consciousness— sometimes confused or contradictory, but great. With more than thirty years' experience of giving spiritual guidance, I know there is truth in Freud's theory about God.

I have met, cared for and, when they were in positions of authority over others, challenged many people whose God was little more than an infantile projection of 'Daddy'—though in most cases it would be truer to say an infantile projection of 'Mummy'. 'Father' was always the gender ascription verbally applied to God, but 'Mummy' more accurately reflects the actual attributes and qualities they gave God.

Nowadays, it is generally recognised that Freud was more than a little bit of a patriarchal, male chauvinist. I suspect this is why he missed the gender issue. After all, it is Mother, not Father, who provides most of the nurturing and protection of the child in infancy. Ascribing male gender to this projected 'Mummy-God' was merely a matter of religious custom and tradition. I have always felt these people suffered from sick religion— or, more correctly, suffered from psychic illness projected through religion. But it is quite a different matter to claim sweepingly, as does Freud, that religion *itself* is sick.

Inevitably, Freud soon received the tit-for-tat his superficial theory deserved. Critics started psychoanalysing Freud himself. They pointed out that, as an atheist, he seemed obsessed with religion: that his own accounts of his dreams were filled with religious figures, symbols and themes; that as a Jew living in a dominantly Christian society his atheism was a reaction to the evils of anti-Semitism; that his denial of God had to do with problems with his parents in his own childhood. And so on.

As a generalisation, Freud's theory of God has so little in it that one could ignore it were it not for the fact that, by process of drip down, it has affected the heirs of his own art and secular society generally. Thanks largely to Freud, psychology and psychiatry still enjoy popular prestige as sciences. Even in universities and courts of law, they tend to be seen as science rather than a skilful art. To maintain this prestige, they are generally wary of matters spiritual, even if they no longer peddle Freud's theory of God.

Jung is Freud's most famous disciple and probably his most able.

He rebelled against core parts of his master's theories, always considering himself a traditional Christian. But Jung is still dismissed by the mainstream of Freud's heirs as a mystic. If you want to maintain the scientific image, it certainly does not do to have a mystical 'cat' among your scientific 'pigeons'! Thus in Western culture, psychiatry and psychology, the official, mainstream legitimators of sanity, are wary of, if not hostile to, religion. It is thus little wonder that publicly there is a widespread proclivity to treat religion as a private sop and crutch.

An extraordinary development of the last thirty years is the way many clergy have adopted, not challenged, the restricted vision of the psychological and psychiatric intellectual club. As their legitimacy in the eyes of secular society has declined, clergy increasingly have carved out a role for themselves as (amateur) counsellors.

For a short time, this strategy might give clergy a modicum of authority in secular eyes, but it digs their own graves as spiritual guides. It makes religion appear more of a sop than ever and reflects its failure to perceive its own vital springs in mystical experiences rather than in rationality and belief. Theophanies, not counselling sessions, are the heart of religion.

✠ The year of thinking dangerously

As I have said, it was during my third year of training for the Anglican priesthood that I became an atheist for several months. That was also the year of what I call my creative insanity.

What the religion of rational intelligence offered a young theological student, himself a product of secular society, was the faith castle. This castle represented the whole edifice of Christian doctrines and ethics. You were invited to leap into it without ever knowing whether it was a mere castle-in-the-air or something solid, such as a castle made of stone and wood.

There were rational intelligence arguments supporting the solid 'stone and wood theory' and there were cancelling counter-arguments supporting the fantasy 'castle-in-the-air' theory. You were advised that it was impossible ever to know which theory accorded with reality and that getting into the castle was a matter of making a leap of faith. If you took the faith-leap, thereafter you were supposed to act 'as if' the castle was solid, even though you could never really know. If you decided not to leap, then you were advised to go and find some other castle or, as most people do today, build sandcastles out of everyday life.

St Augustine of Hippo was invoked as the chief expert in faith-leap castle theory. His saying *Credo ut intelligam* ('I believe in order that I may understand') was given apparent modern respectability by analogy with modern science.

At this time, I was twenty-two years of age. My own experience was not 'I believe in order that I may understand'. It was: 'I know. Please help me to understand how I know and please help me to know more.' I suspect this is the view with which most theological students commence their studies. Here I was in my third year and I was still clinging to it!

The Augustine science faith-castle theory went something like this:

> Everyone has assumptions that they can never prove; they just believe in them. Science, for example, believes the universe is ordered and obeys laws. Scientists investigate the universe in order to discover its underlying order and laws. But the actual scientific assumption of an ordered lawful universe is a starting belief, an unproven matter of faith. But it works.

Scientists do uncover order and laws. It is the same, so this theory goes, with God and Christianity. You take the leap of faith and believe, then you find it actually works.

Even as a twenty-two-year-old I could not accept this. The comparison with science did not make sense. In the first place, everyone, not just professional scientists, accepts that there is a real world 'out there' which is the object of our consciousness. This is not a matter of faith; we know it. I felt I knew the reality of God in the same way. It seemed to me that God did not require a blind leap of faith to be real any more than did the 'external world'.

Science works with quantities— with what can be weighed, measured etc. This is how it establishes the validity of its theories and is able to call them laws. I could not see how the psyche and human consciousness, let alone God, could be investigated quantitatively. The comparison did not hold.

This whole argument, too, ignored the fact that, increasingly, science understands its laws as statistical probabilities. In microphysics, it appears that the building blocks of the 'external world' are a random flux of particles or events. Scientific laws are beginning to look like averages of these chance, chaotic happenings. It was this more modern science that made sense to me, not the analogy with Augustine's 'I believe in order that I may understand'. A universe built from randomness and chaos at its fundamental level makes more sense of a divine intention to create beings such as ourselves, who have a degree of free choice about our lives, than a deterministic, law-driven, mechanistic universe. But that is another story.

At twenty-two, my experience of God was 'I know, but I

want to understand how I know and how to grow in knowing'. The rational-intelligence way of doing theology undermines this knowing and replaces it with belief. Its graduates go out into church and society preaching, 'Take a leap into this faith-castle and you will be saved'.

A raft of reasons are given today to try and persuade you to take this leap, but for every one of them there is an equally convincing counter-argument. This whole approach, unsurprisingly, hardly causes a ripple in secular society today. To the image of religion as a sop for those who need it, there is added the image of a purely subjective faith for those who want to believe in it. Religion, the centre of human life and public society in every other age, becomes a private and closet affair.

At twenty-two, I had neither the confidence nor the understanding to take my 'I know' anywhere. I was confused, empty, feeling on the brink of insanity.

My room at theological college was typical of all the other rooms: very institutional, not dissimilar to the usual university college room. Decoratively, it exhibited a pure devotion to the abstractions of rational intelligence. There was grey carpet, a built-in desk-cum-bookshelf, frosted glass in the window and cream painted walls. Covering the brown iron bed was a chocolate-brown bed cover. On it, stitched in large yellow lettering, were the college initials 'MTC'.

I recall many times during my third year sitting at the desk, looking at the bed and wondering seriously:

> Am I an ordination student in a theological college, or am I
> a mental asylum inmate pretending to myself that I am an
> ordination student in a theological college?

Peer and staff pressure to conform to the communal faith-leap castle was mentally, morally and spiritually invasive.

But it would be cheap and easy to blame my old college. Certainly, I experienced immense emotional and mental pain, so much so that it was ten years before I could bring myself to put a foot in the college door again. But the same would have happened to me in any theological college, whether another Anglican one or even a Catholic or Protestant college. My problem was not with a particular brand of Western theology. My problem, as I see it now, was with any brand of theology that replaced knowing with believing— which, in the twentieth century, perhaps as a consequence of the influence of secular culture, means almost the whole Western church, Anglican, Catholic and Protestant.

Despite its blinkered vision, my four years as a student at Moore College in Sydney were invaluable. Paradoxically, I value it most for its gift of intellectual rigour. So long as you went along with the 'faith-leap castle' theory, the reasoning was lucid and tight. I am grateful, too, that it forced me to take seriously mainstream historic Christianity, not some watered-down, secularised version of it. The fact that it taught believing, not knowing, and frequently verged on fundamentalism, was my problem.

But what I have come to value even more about those college years is the near insanity they produced in me and the fine line of many a year after. One must become quite a bit 'mad' in the compartmentalised world of the sanity of secular-rationalist society if one is to gain any integration at all. As Colin Wilson says:

> . . . the more highly developed the intellect, and the faculty for focussing attention, the more the world is seen as meaningless.

Langdon Gilkey, the American theologian, says human beings can bear just about any amount of pain and suffering so long as they can see a purpose in it. The corollary is that we can't bear much at all if everything appears ultimately meaningless.

Freud held that the purpose of psychoanalysis, his 'talking cure', is not the impossible task of relieving us of all our neuroses. Its purpose, he said, is to restore hysterical patients to the normal range of neuroseis.

But Freud's reduction of the psyche to a scientific object contributes greatly to ultimate meaninglessness. It is not surprising that he came to theorise a death instinct as inherent in the psyche. His explanation of this is that, since we arose out of inorganic matter and (according to Freud the atheist) out of nothing else, we have an inbuilt desire, as it were, to return to it.[1] What Freud needed was a little more madness, not less, for his sanity's sake!

Patrick White explored meaning with his novelist's gifts of imagination and intuitive knowing. He viewed God as his inspirer and intellectuals (by which he meant rationalists) as those who explore only the surface of reality. He hoped his art would help them to see their own unprofessed faith. Though there is irony in what he says about it, Patrick White knew the novelist's journey ran the risk of insanity. In 1970, he wrote the following to Margaret Sumner:

> I suspect I shall go nuts in the end like Barry Humphries.
> At least he is only split in two [his other persona being
> 'Dame Edna Everage'], whereas I shall break into fifteen.[2]

His humour here is ironic. He knew from his artistic success, displayed in the arrogance of his personal relationships, that he possessed a seer's sanity. For him it was those who lived on the surface, the intellectuals, who were crazy— crazy to accept a shallow, unspiritual life as normal. But the fear of madness, as we shall see, had a certain genuine prospect about it for him, too.

Both artistic and mystical insight entail not only a preparedness to be thought crazy by others, but also a preparedness to delve behind social definitions of sanity, searching for deeper levels of reality and meaning. Cowper's famous line, 'Great wits to madness are near allied', is not by any means limited merely to what others think. In a world of closet religion, to 'come out' about one's theophanies is thought mad.

My college insanity drove me deeper. I knew and therefore could not accept either the sanity of the faith-castle or the sanity of secular compartmentalising with its closet religion. But did I know or was I truly mad? Little wits like me must be closer allied to madness when they delve than great wits.

Could I spend my life building sandcastles on the shore of everyday life until the tide came in and washed them away? Could I profess public belief in the scientific world view and privately dismiss its conclusions about meaninglessness as nonsense, holding on to some small grains of religion in my closet? The answer was 'no'.

✠ The craziness of secular sanity

Just as Patrick White suspects that most of us are religious, I suspect most of us know that secular sanity is craziness. But we need, individually and as secular societies, to give ourselves permission to admit the craziness. How else will new levels of integration be found?

One of my closest friendships began when I asked my friend the question: 'What stops you from going mad?' There was a long silence, but still direct eye contact. I broke the silence saying: 'Do you think that is a silly question?'

Her quick reply was: 'If I thought that was a silly question, then I'd think you were a silly man.'

This is a question a disintegrated, compartmentalised, secular mind and society needs to ask. Normally, people do not choose to go mad. It happens to them when they repress, block and split the unity of the self. By the time they have gone mad, they do not know what caused it, let alone have any idea of their own part in it.

Recently my son, a lawyer in his late twenties, told me that a few of his friends had praised him as the most 'together' person they knew. This amused us both greatly. For years, he and I have conversed about the chasms and gorges, cliffs and peaks of consciousness we both explore. His acceptance of his friends' accolade was both appropriate and accurate. He said: 'Maybe it's true. But if I'm more sane, it's only because I know how mad I am.'

Our initial induction into the prevailing social definition of sanity is through family. Given half a chance, Patrick White's family would have ensured his normality— not as an inspired artist, but as a gentleman farmer in the Australian country-gentry tradition. Of his return to Australia after World War II, White says:

> Friends of my parents' generation were sceptical, not to say afraid, of this curious hybrid produced by my mother for their inspection. Though they knew there were novelists in the world because their wives frequented libraries, what could possibly become of an Australian male of their class who set out to be a professional author? My father would be spared

the shame of it. An Australian chauvinist of the old order, he had died in 1937 . . .

I knew more or less before I arrived that my mother and I could not live in the same hemisphere.[3]

In the same letter in which he said he hoped his books might 'give professed unbelievers glimpses of their own unprofessed faith', Patrick White wrote:

The churches defeat their own aims, I feel, through the banality of their approach, and by rejecting so much that is sordid and shocking which can still be related to religious experience.[4]

White's own unsentimental assessment of his family, particularly of his mother, might seem sordid and shocking to many. But Jesus faced the charge of insanity and had to struggle with his family in order to fulfil his destiny. He was not the perfect middle-class son of the perfect middle-class mother so much modern church legend makes him out to be.

For example, St Mark's Gospel tells this little story about him:

He entered a house, and once more such a crowd collected round them that they had no chance even to eat. When his family heard about it, they set out to take charge of him. 'He is out of his mind,' they said.[5]

Social definitions of normality are usually at their most astringent when seeking to control the more powerful forces in our lives. Family is their initial and most persuasive mediator. Sexuality is one such powerful force and spirituality another.

I recall a lecture given at the University of New South Wales in the early 1970s when I was chaplain there. It was delivered by the then president of the Australian and New Zealand College of Psychiatrists. The lecturer gave an hour's worth of reasons why homosexuality was a definable and diagnosable mental disorder.

Twenty-five years later, the definable disorder is not homosexuality, but homophobia. There's been a complete turn-around in society's thinking. Then, as now, no-one knows the causes of homosexuality any more than we know the causes of heterosexuality. Telling your parents you are gay has been the most difficult part of coming out of the closet for most homosexuals, because family has been the chief mediator of social sanity. Telling your parents you are destined to be a novelist or that you have theophanies might outrage family sanity in the same way.

Mary, the mother of Jesus, is legendarily pictured as a model of serene, saintly motherhood. Such a picture ignores the 'sordid and shocking' nature, to use White's terms, of relationships in the Nazareth family as told in the Bible itself. St Mark portrays Mary and the family as out to curb Jesus' sense of his divine destiny in the name of family normality. It is a picture of conflict, not peace:

> Then his mother and his brothers came; and standing outside they sent to him and called him. A crowd was sitting around him; and they said to him, 'Your mother and your brothers and sisters are outside asking for you.' And he replied, 'Who are my mother and my brothers?' And looking at those who sat around him, he said, 'Here are my mother and my brothers. Whoever does the will of God is my brother, sister and mother.'[6]

Patrick White's homosexuality and spirituality conjoined to place him at the margin of society's social definition of sanity. He spoke openly about both only late in life, at age sixty-nine, when his self-portrait *Flaws in the Glass* was published. He knew that his social marginality gave his creative imagination an edge it might otherwise have lacked. It assisted him to imagine himself into the consciousness and feelings of all sorts and conditions of being human, both male and female. Imaginatively, he explored all that was sordid and shocking, sane and deluded, righteous and self-righteous. His art opens up his readers to depths of self excluded by normal sanity.

Writing of this kind of inner journeying, he says:

> I sometimes wonder how I would have turned out had I been born a so-called normal heterosexual male. If an artist, probably a pompous one, preening myself in the psychic mirror for being a success, as did the intolerable Goethe . . . My unequivocal male genes would have allowed me to exploit sexuality to the full. As a father I would have been intolerant of my children, who would have hated and despised me, seeing through the great man I wasn't. I would have accepted titles, orders and expected a state funeral in accordance with a deep-seated hypocrisy I had refused to let myself recognise.
>
> As a woman, I might have been an earth mother, churning out the children I wanted of my husband, passionate, jealous, resentful of the cause and the result, always swallowing the bile of some insoluble frustration. Or I might have chosen a whore's life for its greater range of role-playing, greater than that offered an actress, deluding my male audience of one into thinking I was at his service, then flinging back at him the shreds of his self-importance as he buttoned up. Or else a nun, of milky complexion and sliced-bread smile, dedicated to her quasi-spiritual

marriage with the most demanding spouse of all.

Instead, ambivalence has given me insights into human nature, denied, I believe to those who are unequivocally male or female.[7]

We cannot all live on such an edge as this, but we can share the booty of those who have gone over, done battle and returned. Almost always, they will be artists or mystics.

A good sign that Western culture is beginning to recognise the disease (in the sense of uneasiness) of its fractured identity is the revival of interest in the arts. Even in a country as sport-crazed as Australia, major gallery exhibitions now attract larger attendances than football finals. A better sign of the search for deeper integration would be a renewed interest in mystical religion. But thus far, Western culture has seen only a revival of ancient magic and superstition, cleverly renamed 'New Age'.

Patrick White was first an artist, then a mystic. In his self-portrait, he responded consciously to the oft-repeated charge that he was spiritually vague. What he wrote is beautiful, mystical, disturbing— and vague. Ironically vague. He teases, deliberately, those who expect him to speak of belief and abstraction, not knowledge and experience.

He says:

What do I believe? I am accused of not making it explicit. How to be explicit about a grandeur too overwhelming to express, a daily wrestling match with an opponent whose limbs never become material, a struggle from which the sweat and blood are scattered on the pages of anything the serious writer writes? A belief contained less in what is said than in the silences. In patterns on water. A gust of wind. A flower opening. I hesitate to add a child, because a child can grow into a monster, a destroyer.

Am I a destroyer? This face in the glass which has spent a lifetime searching for what it believes, but can never prove to be, the truth. A face consumed by wondering whether the truth can be the worst destroyer of all.[8]

White denies the validity of his critics' question. What does he believe? He does not so much believe as wrestle and see. If you wish to know what has come out of his wrestling with God, he implies, then read the novels—there you will find it written in sweat and blood. But do those who ask the belief question really know how dangerous, threatening and elusive the truth is? Do they realise it is a matter of suffering, not just thinking?

✠ Jesus the insane mystic

Christianity is an historical, mystical religion of the East. Its founder was, at least initially, thought mad by his family.

So far as we know, he wrote nothing. His first followers, like him, were all Jews. Some of them wrote about him in stories and in letters that now form the New Testament part of the Christian Bible. But several centuries of interpreting these stories and letters through the eyes of Greek metaphysical philosophy, Plato especially, has led to the impression in Western culture that Christianity is a system of doctrines to be believed rather than a way to know and a mysticism to be experienced.

In typical Eastern style, Jesus did not teach a system. He spoke, according to the Gospels, evocatively in proverbs, parables, wisdom sayings and stories. By every account, his sense of God was experiential and direct, not achieved by a leap into a faith-castle. He spoke authoritatively, but refused to invoke authority to justify his authority. His authority resided in seeing, experiencing and knowing, not faith-leap believing. Thus like White, when asked to be explicit, Jesus is enigmatic and teasing:

> When he entered the temple, the chief priests and elders of the people came to him as he was teaching and said, 'By what authority are you doing these things, and who gave you this authority?'
>
> Jesus said to them, 'I will also ask you one question; if you tell me the answer, then I will also tell you by what authority I do these things. Did the baptism of John come from heaven, or was it of human origin?'
>
> And they argued with one another, 'If we say, "From heaven," he will say to us, "Why then did you not believe him?" But if we say, "Of human origin," we are afraid of the crowd; for all regard John as a prophet.' So they answered Jesus, 'We do not know.'
>
> And he said to them, 'Neither will I tell you by what authority I do these things.' [9]

Jesus is an inner-worldly, not an other-worldly, mystic. That is to say, he perceives God in the midst of the world, not through rejection of the world. He lives the spiritual life in the world, too. Harvests, camels, rain, floods, doors, moths, foxes, salt, tax collectors, ears, eyes, dishes, famines, coins, clouds, prostitutes, vineyards, bread, wine, breastfeeding, sun, moon, stars are just some of the 'world stuff' upon which he draws in his sayings and teachings.

Patrick White accuses the churches of banality and 'rejecting so much that is sordid and shocking which can still be related to religious experience'. Such an accusation would not hold against the church's founder. Traitors, prostitutes, wine-bibbers, under-class workers, the leprous, adulteresses, the insane, the fringe dweller, the physically deformed are some among the 'sordid and shocking' for whom Jesus cared.

So-called weirdos, crazies, nothings and outcasts, according to the Gospels, receive his special care. Care such as this could only derive from an imaginative empathy which enables Jesus to view others from within the constructs of their own lives— an incarnation into humanity, not just into the life of a singular man or woman.

It was the divine insanity of Jesus that most rankled society in his day. He wasn't normal. But his was the super-sanity of the great Wit. As it got under the skin of normals, it appeared to them either as a liberation and a grace of healing or a threat to their repression, rigidity and control. The issue of alcohol is an interesting, if unusual, example of this dual response to Jesus.

Abstinence from alcohol was part of the life of a good Christian according to the local church I first joined. Being just seventeen, I naively bought this as part of the spiritual package. Not long afterwards, I refused to eat a pudding made by my mother because it had sherry in it. My parents were not churchgoers, but I thought I was setting a good example! It did not occur to me that according to a story in St John's Gospel, albeit a highly symbolic spiritual story, Jesus turned about seven hundred and fifty litres of water into wine at a marriage feast.

John the Baptist, prophet, eremite and ascetic, was a contemporary forerunner of Jesus. Both were subject to severe censure by their society— though, in the case of alcohol, for opposite reasons. St Luke's Gospel tells the following story of a response by Jesus to such censure:

To what then will I compare the people of this generation, and what are they like? They are like children sitting in the marketplace and calling to one another,

'We played flute for you, and you did not dance; we wailed, and you did not weep.'

For John the Baptist has come eating no bread and drinking no wine, and you say, 'He has a demon'; the Son of Man has come eating and drinking and you say, 'Look, a glutton and a drunkard, a friend of tax collectors and sinners!' Nevertheless, wisdom is vindicated by all her children.[10]

'Son of Man' was Jesus' favourite self-designation. Scholars continue to debate its meaning. It could simply mean 'man' in the generic sense of 'human'. Or it may refer to the apocalyptic Son of Man in the book of Daniel. However Jesus intended the self-designation, his response to censure is clear. He is saying: 'With some people, you just can't win. They are like whingeing kids at play, whining about each other's unfair behaviour. John is ascetic and for that he gets the demon label. I am sociable. I enjoy a good feast and thus the whinge is that I'm a glutton and a drunkard.' Jesus does not deny his wine drinking, but he ascribes the accusation 'drunkard' to others, implying its unfairness.

People don't drink alcohol because it tastes better than other sorts of drink, though it is not uncommon to hear this rationalisation articulated. We drink alcohol for its effects on our consciousness. Some of us drink to numb the pain experienced in ordinary, everyday conciousness—which usually requires ever-increasing quantities. Most of us drink socially for the pleasant effects of what Freud called the 'oceanic feeling', especially the flow of conviviality resulting from decreased emotional inhibition.

As a Jew, Jesus stood in a tradition of ambivalence about alcohol. The Jewish Bible (Christian 'Old Testament') ranges in attitude from condemnation of wine consumption to praising God for the gift of wine given to gladden human hearts. But there is one constancy, true also of the Christian 'New Testament'— drunkenness is outlawed as hostile to the spiritual life.

Defining the difference between being glad-hearted and drunk is not always easy. Modern society requires a definition of drunkenness for road safety. It relies on a quantitative correlation between the concentration of alcohol in the bloodstream and reaction–response times to driving procedures such as brake application.

A definition more appropriate to the spiritual life might be 'passing beyond the point where the drunk self says and does things the sober self would judge immoral'.

Inner-worldly mysticism is risky. It means discerning God and living out the spiritual life in all the messiness of the self, of human relationships and of society— well illustrated, I think, by Jesus' response to alcohol and the response of others to that. Other-worldly mysticism is safer. The world and its messiness is rejected. Needless to say, the two mysticisms result in two very different images of God.

✠ The attempt of normals to impose 'sanity' on Jesus

After Jesus' death, his followers spent several centuries in sometimes acrimonious debate about who he really was. Essentially, it was a fight about retaining his inner-worldly mysticism or rejecting it for other-worldly mysticism.

In that era, Greek philosophy was the dominant way of thinking just as secular rationalism is today. So the debate centred on the nature of Jesus himself, his being. The other-worldly mystics argued that Jesus was never really a human being as such. That was too messy a view to be properly spiritual. They contended that Jesus was an appearance of God in the mere outer shell of a human being.

The inner-worldly mystics insisted that Jesus' life and being was totally human and totally spiritual. They contended that the life of Jesus brought God and the messiness of the world together— that Jesus exhibited the nature and essence of God and the nature and essence of what human beings are and can be. In time, the inner-worldly mystics prevailed in this debate and Jesus' own 'God in the midst of life' mysticism won the day.

Almost immediately, things started to go wrong with the side which won the formal debate. In order to preserve their victory, substance and reality were replaced by formula and words. The dual nature of Jesus, as both human and divine, instead of being an expression of the union between God and the world, God and life, God and humanity, became a mere dogma— a test of spiritual correctness. Gradually, inner-worldly mysticism was replaced by faith-leap dogma saying such things as, 'Believe in Jesus as fully human and fully divine and you will be saved'. But what the inner-worldly mystics had fought for was the actual union of God and the world, not just belief in it. They saw in Jesus an example of that unity. The debate which they had won, and was so soon corrupted, was about life, not just belief. Do you find God in life? Do you have to reject life to find God? Do you need to reject God to find life? These were the critical issues.

What I have been talking about, of course, is known as the Christian doctrine of the incarnation: the two natures, divine and human, in the one person Jesus Christ. We need to see what a travesty of the religion of Jesus it is to turn this doctrine into a matter of faith-leap belief. The question of incarnation is about living and experiencing, about drinking wine and not drinking wine, about life denial or life affirmation, about the nature of being human and about the nature of God. What is at stake is experiencing, not just believing.

As a statement, a formula, the doctrine preserves the inner-worldly mysticism taught and lived by Jesus. He is a unique confluence of God and humanity. There has never been another one like him. My difficulty is not with this belief (though its Greek philosophical format which I have avoided is alien to our way of thinking today), but how the belief has come to be used. To make 'belief' the critical issue is like making maps more important than tracks for bushwalkers. Maps are based on reality, not the other way round.

Inner-worldly mysticism as lived and taught by Jesus contin-ues, too, to be threatened by other-worldly mysticism. I am not referring to the other religions of the East, though some of them are totally given over to other-worldly mysticism, but to a threat from within the Christian movement itself.

When my first church insisted on total abstinence from alcohol, it was giving the nod to other-worldly mysticism. Alco-hol, it was saying, is dangerous to the spiritual life: avoid it. I have no dispute with the warning of danger, but every dispute with the notion that abstinence is the better path to God. Avoidance is safe—but it keeps us naive and childish. It is the same with sex (an even greater fear of other-worldly mystics)—or food, relationships, money or power.

Inner-worldly mysticism, discerning God in the midst of life, is always more dangerous. It offers the possibility of greater integration as well as the danger of disintegration. But only inner-worldly mysticism offers accessibility to adult innocence. Along the way, much that is, in Patrick White's language, 'sordid and shocking' will need spiritual transformation.

✠ Discerning God in the midst of the sordid and the shocking

I myself have been drunk a number of times. I do not just mean drunk in the road safety sense, but in the spiritual sense, too— a drunken self that said and did things my sober self was ashamed of. It is not a state I enjoy or wish to promote. But I do enjoy alcohol's positive alterations to normal consciousness, especially the relaxed, dreamy conviviality it creates.

Mere memory of the things I have said and done when drunk is painful. I certainly have no desire to repeat them. Yet without these episodes, there is insight into self and others I would not have. This is not to advocate the pursuit of drunkenness or other forms of destructive behaviour in order to gain insight! An intentional approach of that kind invites disintegration. What is implied is that the pursuit of inner-worldly mysticism entails the real possibility of taking false tracks. It also implies that the grace of God can turn those false tracks into meaningful journeys.

In my less guarded moments, I like to think of myself as a person of reasonable verbal facility. One of my very close friends thinks no less deeply or broadly than I, but is slower and more careful in articulation. When drunk, I become verbally belligerent, shamefully and outrageously so. On one occasion this friend, completely exasperated by my drunken verbal aggression, left the dining table, went out into the garden, grabbed the garden hose, brought it into my dining room, spraying at full pressure, and gave me and half my furniture a thorough soaking.

Drunkenness has revealed to me the thin patina, the veneer-like quality of my self-image as . . . morally good, sexually integrated, caring, reliable, thoughtful. It exposed this identity as skin, not soul, deep. Soul deep was something uglier: arrogant, selfish, aggressive, exploitative — adult, but not innocent. Most of all, it revealed my level of self-integration as shallow. As I normally attributed to God my sense of 'having it all together', my image of God was exposed as idolatrous.

Drunkenness opened for me the depths of what Carl Jung calls the 'Shadow' self. Jung sees no possibility of human salvation unless the Shadow (or Dark) self is integrated with the Light self. From drunkenness, I could see that Jung is correct to claim that the Shadow contains light, not just darkness— good, not just evil.

Of course, a true light can't shine from the darkness unless it is invited. Neither drunkenness nor other actings-out of the sordid and the shocking are integrative in themselves: quite the opposite. In spiritual terms, God's grace can be resisted. Indeed, it is grace *because* it can be resisted.

This is well known to Alcoholics Anonymous, the most successful movement for integrating those who have fallen into alcoholic disintegration. The AA program does not even begin to work until the alcoholic is willing to call upon the grace of what AA calls a Higher Power.

Much hard work had to go into repairing relationships after my drunken episodes. When it was done, those relationships became firmer and closer than ever. Harder, ongoing work had to go into finding a more inclusive integration of self—and of self and God.

Patrick White speaks movingly about his alcoholic arguments with Manoly Lascaris. Each always felt a false sense of embarrassment in the eyes of the other about their respective countries: Australia for White, Greece for Lascaris. Of visits to Greece, White says:

> Over and over, during these journeys and after, when M tells me I hate Greece, I cannot explain my love. Again, in our more bitter, alcoholic arguments in the kitchen after the evening meal, when he tells me I hate him, I cannot prove that what I believe in most deeply, the novels for which my conscious self can't take full responsibility, our discomforting but exhilarating travels through Greece, our life together, its eruptions and rewards, my own clumsy wrestling with what I see as a religious faith—that all of this is what keeps me going.[11]

Such a confession is almost sentimental for White. One senses a sustaining truth and force of relationship in his honesty about bitter, alcoholic arguments in the kitchen after dinner—an open self of inner-worldly mysticism, not a shut off, repressed self of other-worldly mysticism. Not the daytime sanity of rational reason, either.

✠ True wisdom, the key to true sanity

With or without alcohol's loosening of emotional inhibition, self-truth does not always sustain relationships. It may break them, too. A few beers or a bottle of wine may be a good way to sit down and sort out some problems with a partner or friend. Equally, it may magnify the problems and lead to verbal or physical

violence. As Jesus said when confronted with the accusation
'glutton and drunkard':

Wisdom is vindicated by all her children.

'Wisdom' was no throw away word for Jesus. Wisdom is
feminine gender and, in Jewish understanding, so closely represented God that it was personified. In the book of Proverbs,
the personification of Wisdom allows her to say with her own
voice:

The Lord created me at the beginning of his work,
the first of his acts of long ago.
Ages ago I was set up at the first,
before the beginning of the earth.
When there were no depths, I was brought forth . . .
When he marked out the foundations
of the earth,
then I was beside him, like a master worker;
and I was daily his delight,
rejoicing before him always,
rejoicing in his inhabited world
and delighting in the human race.
And now, my children, listen to me:
happy are those who keep my ways.
Hear instruction and be wise,
and do not neglect it.
Happy is the one who listens to me,
watching daily at my gates,
waiting beside my doors.
For whoever finds me finds life
and obtains favour from the Lord;
but those who miss me injure themselves;
all who hate me love death.[12]

According to Jesus, it matters not whether one is called mad or bad, demonic or drunkard, for Wisdom, not social opinion, is the criterion of worth. And she is vindicated by her children. She is the mother of all knowing. Rational intelligence is just part of her.

To substitute reason for Wisdom is to dismember and disfigure her. She is art and religion, not just science and philosophy. She alone is sanity and life; all else is madness and death.

4.

Mystery

The re-enchantment of self and life

I SPOKE IN THE PREVIOUS CHAPTER ABOUT THE EFFECTS of alcohol on self-perception. No-one, so far as I know, has ever suggested that alcohol can induce theophanies. Drunks might see pink elephants or, when sobered-up, see themselves more deeply, but they do not see God.

Yet a claim to experience theophany is actually made for the effects of hallucinogenic drugs.

✠ Aldous Huxley, William James and drug-induced mysticism

The most sophisticated, most compelling, most articulate of these claims is Aldous Huxley's in his book, *The Doors of Perception.* Huxley experimented with mescalin in the early 1950s. Publication of his book instigated a virtual fad of serious experimentation. It could be said that this fad lasted well into the 1970s with the advocacy of LSD by Alan Watts, Timothy Leary and others.

Huxley was a highly cerebral intellectual. Mescalin, the effects of which last approximately eight hours, completely altered his view of the 'real world'. He claimed his mescalin experience was equivalent to the salvation sought by religion through spiritual mysticism:

> I continued to look at the flowers and, in their living light, I seemed to detect the qualitative equivalent of breathing— but of a breathing without returns to a starting-point, with no recurrent ebbs, but only a repeated flow from beauty to heightened beauty, from deeper to ever deeper meaning. Words like 'Grace' and 'Transfiguration' came to mind and this, of course, was what, among other things, they stood for.
>
> My eyes travelled from the rose to the carnation, and from that feathery incandescence to the smooth scrolls of sentient amethyst which were the iris. The Beatific Vision, Sat Chit Ananda, Being-Awareness-Bliss— for the first time I understood, not on a verbal level, not by inchoate hints or at a distance, but precisely and completely what these prodigious syllables referred to.[1]

Huxley's experience is well known. But not all mescalin experimenters had Huxley's positive experience. The French philosopher, Sartre, underwent a nightmarish experience of being chased by lobster-like monsters. R.C. Zaehner, an Oxford professor of Eastern religions, was simply consumed by hysterical laughter.

Those whose mescalin experience was negative wrote in warning against Huxley's advocacy of the grace of the drug. What follows is part of an article published in the *Manchester Guardian* by the subject of a controlled scientific experiment:

> My claim to comment on these adventurous proposals is that I, too, have acted as a guinea-pig for scientists investigating

mescalin and have shared Mr Huxley's revelation, though in another form. The drug caused him to see our normal world transfigured and made profoundly more significant. It pitch-forked me into an inner world, overwhelming and different in kind from that mediated to us by our senses. Are we all, I wonder, quite ready for that? . . .

Mescalin, it will be remembered, induces a temporary condition of schizophrenia, but it cannot be predicted what form this will take for any particular person.[2]

Part of this guinea-pig's fearful experience is reported this way:

I seemed to be caught like a wasp in the sordid brown treacle of man's anger. I saw a wild black figure chopping off heads, because it was so funny to see them fall. Worst of all, I came across the 'lost', squatting grey-veiled, among grey rooks, 'at the bottom', unable to communicate alone beyond despair . . .

I do not feel I could have survived much longer, without the protective covering of my own little ego, but for the appearance of a celestial female figure. She did not seem to be linked with any particular religion. I described her as 'coming out of the gold, clothed in soft blues and purples, infinitely benign and compassionate . . . like a pearl coming into a world of diamond . . .' She was gay, with a gaiety no scherzo can even hint at, and she laughed at me and said, 'You were being shown the universe before the principle of communication, which is love, has been injected into it. Now, you see the next job.'[3]

The fad of serious experimentation with hallucinogenic drugs has dropped away, swallowed up by recognition of the destructive effects and addictions of escapist abusers. It left one lasting value. To cerebral intellectuals such as Huxley, it demonstrated experientially the confined, limited perceptions of ordinary, everyday, rational consciousness. It convinced Huxley that religion spoke not only of the real, but of the more real. It might be said, though, that Huxley was predisposed to see what he saw—that in some sense he *created* it. His deliberate experimentation does suggest he was looking for something more than the meaninglessness produced by cerebral abstraction or a religion of mere words.

This was not the case with William James. James, too, was cerebral—the epitome of the detached scientific observer cautiously seeking to comprehend the workings of the psyche. James was not expecting anything in particular from his nitrous oxide experiment. What he did experience came as a surprise and left him permanently changed, with a new view of self and world.

You will recall from chapter 2 that part of what he said afterwards was:

> One conclusion was forced upon my mind at that time and my impression of its truth has ever since remained unshaken. It is that our normal waking consciousness, rational consciousness as we call it, is but one special type of consciousness, whilst all about it, parted from it by the flimsiest of screens, there lie potential forms of consciousness entirely different.[4]

Most significantly, and a matter to which we will return shortly, James says of drug-induced experiences of expanded consciousness that they 'open a region though they fail to give a map'.

For Christian theology and mysticism, the ecstatic Beatific Vision, which Huxley thought he saw under mescalin, is the experience of final salvation—from sin, guilt, meaninglessness and despair. It comes (or does not come) as we pass through death to God.

✠ St Paul and mystic revelation

As we saw in chapter 1, St Paul's religion was founded upon an experience of mystic revelation: his Damascus Road theophany. St Paul always remained a mystic: a mystic of the Spirit of God which sometimes he calls 'the Holy Spirit' or 'the Spirit of Christ'. However, thanks to Western faith-castle theology, St Paul has been turned into a rationalistic abstract theologian whose teachings are merely to be believed. For Paul himself, it is not belief but the Spirit's gift of knowing that is central to his religion.

At the first-century Greek city of Corinth, Paul faced a gathering of Christ's followers who were out and out ecstatics. They were captivated by glossolalia or 'speaking in tongues'. This is a phenomenon that appears from time to time in different religions. Some were using wine as a stimulant to their worship ecstasies. Paul reminded them that Jesus inaugurated the use of wine in eucharistic worship— not as a stimulant, but as a symbol of his blood shed in death. Like Huxley, the Corinthians were equating their ecstasy with salvation itself. Paul challenged this equation in two ways.

First, he argued, keeping in mind the life of Christ as an example, that the test of valid spiritual experience is love, not ecstasy:

> If I speak in the tongues of mortals and of angels, but do not have love, I am a noisy gong or a clanging cymbal. And if I have prophetic powers, and understand all mysteries and all knowledge, and if I have all faith, so as to remove mountains, but do not have love, I am nothing.[5]

There is a fascinating parallel here, you will notice, with the report of the *Manchester Guardian*'s mescalin 'guinea-pig'. In that account, the guinea-pig is rescued from disintegration by a celestial female figure who says: 'You were being shown the universe before the principle of communication, which is love, has been injected into it. Now, you see the next job.'

To the inner-worldly mysticism of Jesus, there never was a time when the principle of love was absent from the universe. He lived and taught that God is love. But the parallel with the drug-induced experience is fascinating all the same.

Second, St Paul challenged the Corinthian equation of ecstasy and ultimate salvation by comparing our limited vision of life now with the Beatific Vision to come:

> Love never ends. But as for prophecies, they will come to an end; as for tongues, they will cease; as for knowledge, it will come to an end. For we know only in part, and we prophesy only in part; but when the complete comes, the partial will come to an end.
>
> When I was a child, I spoke like a child, I thought like a child, I reasoned like a child; when I became an adult, I put an end to childish ways. For now we see in a mirror, dimly, but then we shall see face to face. Now, I know only in part; then, I will know fully, even as I have been fully known.[6]

✠ Drug experimentation and the failure of the Western church

As we saw, Huxley equated his mescalin 'vision' with the Beatific Vision: '. . . for the first time I understood, not on a verbal level, not by inchoate hints or at a distance, but precisely and completely what those prodigious syllables referred to.'

Later, in his book's epilogue, Huxley qualified this view saying: 'I am not so foolish as to equate what happens under the influence of mescalin or of any other drug, prepared or in the future preparable, with the realisation of the end and ultimate purpose of life: enlightenment, the Beatific Vision.'

He says that mescalin ecstasy should be valued only as a helpful insight into, or a foretaste of, the real thing. It should be seen as: '. . . what Catholic theologians call a "gratuitous grace", not necessary to salvation but potentially helpful and to be accepted thankfully, if made available.'[7]

This alone is the lasting legacy of the fad which saw cerebral intellectuals experimenting seriously with hallucino-genic drugs. It revealed the limitations of rational consciousness and something, maybe only an imitation, of the reality which religion knows. It was William James, though, who saw the critical issue. He understood that merely opening the floodgate of consciousness supplied no salvation because, in his words, 'it failed to give a map'.

Failure to find a map is probably why the insights derived from drug experimentation didn't lead anywhere. 'No maps' was also the warning voiced by the *Manchester Guardian* guinea-pig. So, though people such as William James and Aldous Huxley discovered vast territories of being and consciousness, the ultimate impact on secular culture was nil.

In large part, this must be explained by the mystical failure of the Western church. Seeking to maintain its credibility in a rational-intelligence culture, it has turned theology into an exercise in maps, not territory. That is to say, it is an exercise in drawing up a system of logical, coherent beliefs which do not seem to relate to anything. Theology becomes words, not experience— a belief system which invites acceptance through a leap of faith. By substituting belief for mystical experience, the truth of the maps is turned into abstract dogma. Spiritual experience is replaced by spiritual authority. The church's truth becomes the authority of the church—take it or leave it. The Bible's truth becomes the authority of the Bible—take that, too, or leave it.

Or, worse still, as in the case of Patrick White, theology becomes the trivia of a ban against bean-jar guessing competitions. In such circumstances, it is little wonder that religion and experiences of theophany get locked away in our private closets.

✠ Patrick White and mystic revelation

Patrick White did not class himself among the cerebral intellectuals. But he was acutely aware of the issue of maps and spiritual territory. Eighteen months after his slip-in-the-mud theophany, he said:

> I have not myself suffered any of the great injustices, such as hunger, or torture, or the devastations of war, to name a few, but I do feel by this time that all the minor injustices to which I have been submitted, and which at the time have seemed terribly unjust and unnecessary, even agonising, have in fact been necessary to my development. I do feel that every minute of my life has been necessary—though this conviction has only very recently come to me—and that the sum total can only be good, though how good one cannot presume to say.
>
> None of this is new. It is quite simple. You may even find it ludicrous. But it is better to say it, in case it may help simply by its simplicity and obviousness. I think it is impossible to explain faith. It is like trying to explain air, which one cannot do by dividing it into its component parts and labelling them scientifically. It must be breathed to be understood.

But breathing is something that has been going on all the time, and is almost imperceptible. I do not know when I began to have faith, but it is only a short time since I admitted it.[8]

More than twenty years later, White was still affirming the experiential, spiritual vision which came to focus in his 1951 slip-in-the-mud theophany. By now he had had plenty of occasion to reflect on it, to question it, to doubt it. But it remained foundational—a stubborn, recalcitrant experience. In 1973 he wrote:

I also have a belief in a supernatural power of which I have been given inklings from time to time: there have been incidences and coincidences which have shown me that there is a design behind the haphazardness. I suppose there is one line of thought which would say I see it because I want to, but from my teens to middle age I didn't want to: it was only when it was forced on me that I had to accept.[9]

White knew the reality of spiritual territory, but he never did quite find the map to guide him in it.

I met Patrick White only once, in 1983. As I have mentioned, after my 'St George's light theophany', Eremos was founded. Two friends, Colin Alcock and Don Meadows, founded it with me. We wanted White to speak at an Eremos meeting. Colin wrote to him and we were invited to his home, opposite Centennial Park in Sydney, to discuss the possibility. *Flaws in the Glass*, White's self-portrait, had not long been published. In it, he voiced some sharp criticisms of the Church, of Christianity and, especially, of Anglicans. Yet from his novels, with their haunting mysticism of person, place and object, we knew Patrick White was a spiritual person.

However, we were nervous about the reception we might receive. *Flaws in the Glass* reserved some of its sharpest barbs for Anglicans of the Sydney Diocese and Don and I were rectors of Sydney parishes at the time. I was personally nervous because, from his novels, I knew what a discerning person White was. I thought he might peer into my soul's depths and not find much there.

He answered the door in response to our knock. Some of my nervousness took flight as, briefly, we viewed and discussed the icons adorning the entranceway to the house. I, fortunately, had long ago ditched the uninformed Protestant view that the Eastern Orthodox love of icons was a form of idolatry, involving the worship of pictures. I had come to appreciate Eastern Christianity's view of the icon as a way of mystically experiencing God through contemplation of the material and the artistic. Thus, icons could soothe nerves. But I was unprepared for the great contrast of the living room into which we were ushered. This was dominated by, what seemed on the day, the garish sensuality of some huge Brett Whiteley paintings.

White gestured that we sit on soft pale lounge-chairs. There was silence. The usually voluble Eremos trio sat dumbstruck, not knowing how to begin. White was sombre. Even when greeting us at the front door, he had not smiled. It was he who broke the silence: 'I don't know why you've come to see me about giving a talk. I'm not a Christian, you know.'

At the time I could not have said why, but I knew this was a test. If we failed it, then I guessed we might be shown the door rather smartly or that things might get rough for us verbally. I can recall my reply exactly. I said: 'Mr White, it surprises me to hear you say that you are not a Christian. From your novels, I would have thought that you were very much a Christian.'

What the test was never became clear. Afterwards, we wondered about it. Was it a moral test? Did we know about his homosexuality? As Sydney Anglicans, would we accept a homosexual as a Christian? (We did not in fact hold the standard 'love the sinner, hate the sin' view.) Was it something else? Was White just being honest with us? Or was it a test of substance: to see whether we were just 'simple believers'? We didn't know.

Whatever the test was, we passed it. Patrick White relaxed and smiled. We stayed several hours, were introduced to the dogs, helped make tea in the kitchen and ate homemade cake in the back garden. White declined to accept the Eremos invitation, explaining a self-imposed limitation to speak publicly only on the nuclear disarmament issue.

It was puzzling that White did not seek to refute or challenge my claiming him for the Christian fold. Perhaps it was simply that we had passed the test and nothing else mattered. But, as we shall see, White was forever ambivalent about himself and Christianity. A few weeks after our visit he wrote to me, articulating this ambivalence and confirming a continuing search for a valid map of spiritual territory:

> One of the Merton books which has impressed me most is his *Mystics and Zen Masters*. A friend lent it and I am now trying to get hold of copies to give, but it seems to be out of print. I feel the link between Christianity and Eastern beliefs is most important today, particularly in Australia where so many people are wary of orthodox church religion. Myself for instance.

Here, I think, 'orthodox church religion' means for White the religion of Christ presented as a system of doctrines to be believed (the 'faith castle') and moral rules to be obeyed. His own spirituality was grounded in theophany, experience and intuitive insight. By reading people like Merton, he was looking to learn from those who know, not merely believe. Ten years after his slip-in-the-mud theophany, White said of his own churchgoing:

> I made the attempt, found that churches destroy the mystery
> of God, and had to evolve symbols of my own through
> which to worship.[10]

It was not, in fact, as simple as this. Nothing about White's spirituality is simple. In a later chapter, we shall see that White had access, and knew he had access, to an interpretation of Christ's religion capable of providing a map to further fulfil his spiritual desire. We shall see, too, that White had a personal obstacle to Christ's religion in his own character which, possibly, he failed to address with full self-truth.

But his disillusionment with a Christianity that destroys the mystery of God is one I share. His interest in the other religions of the East, with their emphasis on experience and enlightenment, is understandable. This is a popular road for church-disillusioned Westerners to travel. But it never seems, properly, to have occurred to White that Christianity itself is a mystical religion of the East.

✠ The mystical basis of all religion

At base, there are only two forms of religion. Both are mystical in the sense that they are founded in actual experience, not abstract belief.

On the one hand, there is the mysticism of the impersonal. With this mysticism, salvation is attained through loss of self in mystical union with ultimate reality. This is the mysticism of non-theistic Buddhism and Hinduism.

I use the term 'ultimate reality' rather than 'God' because, for many people, the latter automatically connotes personality of some kind. For impersonal mysticism, ultimate reality is beyond any distinction between good and evil. Normal moral terms do not apply. The mystical union that comes from loss of self is bliss, at-one-ness, nirvana. It is achieved through meditational practices and techniques. Impersonal mysticism tends to be other-worldly, sometimes totally other-worldly.

On the other hand, there is the mysticism of the personal. Salvation here is attained by union of the self with God in love. Ultimate reality is personal in the sense that it is conscious of itself, is purposive, is relational and is love. (This is not the same as saying that ultimate reality is a person in the human sense of an individual person.) The human self is not lost in mystical dissolution with ultimate reality, but is fulfilled in a relationship of loving unity.

For the mysticism of the personal, God is good, not beyond good and evil. When God's purpose for creation is fulfilled, evil will cease to exist and only the good will remain. Mystical union in love is achieved by grace alone— or by grace plus human moral goodness. Personal mysticism is the religion of the majority of Buddhists, some Hindus and the followers of the Eastern religions of the Bible— Judaism, Christianity and Islam. Personal mysticism can be either inner-worldly or other-worldly.

This summary is, of course, a simplification. But even acknowledging the many qualifications and exceptions a detailed analysis would require, it is, I believe, valid in the broad sweep. It demonstrates that the popular idea that all religious maps lead to the same destination is false. This view, commonly espoused in the secular West, is based on profound ignorance of the major spiritual maps themselves and is usually voiced by people who follow none. It also shows the falsity of the popular distinction between Eastern and Western religion. Personal mysticism knows no such divide—it is both Eastern and Western.

Throughout the world, most of those who do actually interpret their spiritual lives through the map of one or other of the world religions are mystics of the personal. In this special sense only, it is actually true to say that most religious practice is headed in the same direction.

✠ 'Is ultimate reality personal?': the fundamental question

In this book, it is not my intention to compare religious maps. My intention is, rather, to explore the personal, inner-worldly mysticism of the religion of Jesus as a spiritual experience. Otherwise, Western culture now seems faced with nothing much else to choose from except the meaninglessness of life seen through the eyes of secular rationalism or the faith-castle leap into abstract doctrines so typical of current Western Christianity.

'Is ultimate reality personal?' is a much more sensible and concrete question than rationalism's 'Does God exist?' It immediately negates those standard pictures of God as a superman or superwoman 'out there' somewhere. It recognises that there is some kind of ultimate base or source to everything, but asks, 'What is it like?' rather than, 'Does it exist?' The latter question now looks like a foolish semantic confusion—which is why debates about the existence of God end up nowhere.

If we substitute the term 'ultimate reality' for 'God', then even the twentieth-century's most prominent atheist, the philosopher

Bertrand Russell, had a God. His God was impersonal matter. For Russell, this God promised only damnation in the final triumph of black oblivion over the personal, conscious human self. His God was an enemy, with no salvation possible from its damnable destruction—though Russell himself did seek a kind of salvation by adopting an attitude of heroic defiance and moral superiority in the face of his impersonal ultimate reality.

Yet if you strip away his purple prose and view only his core meaning, Russell's defiance of his God sounds like a mouse squeak in a cyclone:

> Brief and powerless is man's life; on him and on all his race the slow, sure doom falls pitiless and dark. Blind to good and evil, reckless of destruction, omnipotent matter rolls on its relentless way; for man condemned today to lose his dearest, tomorrow himself to pass through the gate of darkness, it remains only to cherish, ere the blow fall, the lofty thoughts that ennoble his little day; disdaining the coward terrors of the slave of Fate, to worship at the shrine that his own hands have built; undismayed by the empire of chance, to preserve a mind free from the wanton tyranny that robs his outward life; proudly defiant of the irresistible forces that tolerate, for a moment, his knowledge and his condemnation, to sustain alone, a weary but unyielding Atlas, the world that his own ideals have fashioned despite the trampling march of unconscious power.[11]

This was written in 1903. If instead of reading 'omnipotent matter', we read 'space–time–matter–energy–universe', then this is the public orthodoxy of scientific rationalism, the world view of those who limit consciousness to secular rational intelligence.

✠ Personal mysticism and postmodern relativism

Russell lived in the period we now call 'the modern era'. Today, we are said to live in 'the postmodern era'. For so-called post-modernists, Russell's simple 'atheism' is out. What is 'in' is a cynical, seemingly tolerant relativism where all spiritual maps, no matter how badly drafted, are as good as each other. Spirituality is not only a topic for the closet, but also a topic of pure subjectivity.

From 1970 to 1975, I was the Anglican chaplain to the University of New South Wales, then Australia's largest university. I took advantage of this appointment to study a new field, completing a degree in sociology. One of my tutors, a person I especially liked (I think because of the suffering compassion I saw in his eyes), espoused total relativism.

'Truth is only your truth or my truth,' he would argue. 'There is no truth as such; everything is relative' (except this claim apparently!). He had the same view of morality. 'Good is only what you happen to like and evil what you dislike,' he would say. 'There is no objective morality, just your good and evil and my good and evil. Everything is subjective.'

One day, he was speaking in this vein to a small class of about a dozen students. Feigning rage and without warning, I rushed across the room, picked up a chair and made as if to hit him over the head with it. He ducked under a table and yelled, 'Don't do that'. 'Why?' I asked insistently. 'Why?' Ever consistent, and I think waking up to my real intentions, he replied, 'Because I wouldn't like it'. We both began to smile. By now, he clearly recognised my purposes were metaphysical, not physical. Nothing more was said. The point had been made.

None of us actually *lives* as if morality is merely a matter of personal likes and dislikes, of boos and hurrahs. We all appeal to notions such as fairness, justice and rights, especially when someone acts against us. We know instinctively that there is a real difference between right and wrong, good and evil. The fact that today we are more than ever aware that moral values vary from age to age and culture to culture does not justify the subjective absurdity of total relativism. It should only make us humble and cautious about identifying our own moral judgments with full moral truth.

It is the same with truth itself. If my sociology tutor was correct—that there is no objectivity, only 'my truth' and 'your truth'—this would put an end not just to all science, art and religion, but to conversation as well. Meaningful talk would be impossible. Each of us would be locked up in our own little subjective world.

Conversation, science, art and religion all require recognition of objective truth—a shared reality of some kind. Again, the fact that today we are more than ever aware that what people take to be truth varies from age to age and culture to culture does not justify the self-contradiction called 'absolute relativism'. It should only make us humble and cautious about identifying the truth as we understand it with absolute truth itself.

Personal mysticism attributes the knowledge of absolute truth to God alone. All our understanding, therefore, is always relative. We never can, and never will, know as God knows. But truth itself is not relative. It is our *understanding* of truth that is relative. It would be clearer, perhaps, to say 'limited' rather than 'relative'. Compared with God, our knowledge of truth is always limited. Only God's consciousness contains all truth.

When, as in the case of modern secular society, religion becomes a purely private affair, locked away in closets without public conversation, it atrophies and regresses to something stunted and immature, even infantile. This is not exactly what happened to Patrick White, but his spiritual journey was impeded by 'going private'. He lost accessibility to adequate guiding maps.

✠ A personal account of spiritual awakening

My own spiritual consciousness, so far as I am aware, did not grow out of any religious teaching, but from the direct experience of self and world— more like the way we learn to breathe or talk than the way we learn to read or write. My first clear memory of its awakening is as a seven-year-old at infants school.

Boys in my co-ed school had divided into two warring gangs. Our playground was not artificially surfaced. The gangs would gather at separate ends of it and the 'brave' would run across grass, sand and rough dirt to punch, throw stones or chuck rotten fruit at members of the opposing gang. Each gang had a separate running track. One day, I managed to conceal some sharp pieces of broken glass in the sand of the opposition's track. I do not know how I achieved this. Possibly, I had run a teacher's errand during class time and did it then. But I did it.

In a working-class Sydney suburb of those days, many children came to school barefoot as their families could not afford to buy shoes. Most boys, anyway, took their shoes off for the gang-runs against the opposition. During gang warfare at lunch time that day, a boy cut his feet terribly on the glass I had placed in the sand. He was taken to hospital, was away from school for several days and his feet were bandaged for some weeks. There were no enquiries. Everyone assumed the glass had got there accidentally. I kept the awful truth to myself.

Inside, my remorse and guilt were overwhelming. I do not remember thinking about God at all, but I knew I had done something dreadful—not just against the injured boy, though that was horrible and personally devastating, but against right order itself. I felt I had perverted some great truth. As a seven-year-old, this was a feeling, not something I could put into words. Whatever innocence I had had was shattered for good. It was the first profound awakening of moral conscience in me.

I do not think I became conscious of God until I was eleven or twelve years old—some time during my last year of primary school. I had, of course, heard plenty of *talk* about God. There were weekly religious education classes at school—'Scripture' it was called—conducted by one of the local clergy. But God didn't mean anything to me—just a word.

With the first stirrings of puberty at about twelve, I began to be aware of my separate existence as a knowing consciousness. Frequently, on scraps of paper I would write out my address. Friends say they did the same about this age. First would be my name, then my house number, the street, the suburb, the city, my state, my country 'Australia', followed by 'the world' and lastly 'the universe'.

Invariably, my thoughts would then wander off into a favourite reverie about space travel. This was more than twenty years before the Russian cosmonaut, Yuri Gagarin, became the first human space traveller.

'Suppose,' I would muse, 'you took off into space in any direction from earth; could your journey ever end?' I would then imagine my spaceship encountering a very prosaic brick wall and would think, 'Either this brick wall goes on forever or, if I can smash through it, "forever" is on the other side of it.'

These boyish reflections mark my first consciousness of that great double reality— self and other. They were the first recognition that consciousness is always consciousness of something or other. Ever after this time I knew there were two realities. On the one hand, there is the feeling, thinking, imagining 'I'. On the other hand, there is what the 'I' thinks, feels and imagines about— anything from planets and brick walls to dreams and visions. But what was this 'I', this personal, knowing self?

As an eleven- or twelve-year-old, I began to think for the first time that just as my body, my physical self, was part of the 'external universe', my 'I' must be part of something bigger, too: something as great in comparison to my tiny 'I' as the universe is great in comparison with my tiny body. I am not sure when I began to think of the greater 'I' as God, but it was soon after.

Thus for me, awareness of God grew simply with awareness of self and world. It was never a matter of believing, but always of seeing, understanding and knowing. Apart from my unsuccessful attempt at theological college to become an atheist, the only doubts I have had about knowing God's reality came during secondary school.

I cannot recall how, but I came to believe that Christianity insisted on taking literally the Genesis story about God creating the universe in six days. Other evidence convinced me this was not so, that the universe was millions of years in the making. I had no idea then that the Genesis story is in the style of Hebrew poetry. But believing I was comparing spiritual apple with scientific apple, it seemed to me that the spiritual one was rotten and that, maybe, my intuitive, knowing God was illusory.

A science teacher helped me to see that the comparison was

not apple to apple, but apple to banana and that creation and evolution were compatible. At this time, I was not a follower of the religion of Jesus but, unknowingly, I had learnt already the importance of Meister Eckhart's saying that, 'If your image of God and the truth part company, then follow the truth and let your image of God catch up'.

Apart from this high school episode, I have never doubted the reality of the 'Great I' behind the 'little I' which is us. I have, of course, doubted whether God is good, whether God is loving or whether God is cruel and indifferent to our pain and suffering. This will be an issue to explore in subsequent chapters.

✠ The absurdity of rational atheism to the mystic

Mystical intelligence knows God directly. To mystical intelligence, it makes no more sense to debate the existence of God than to debate the existence of one's own consciousness and its contents. All are the given realities of being alive as a human being. Atheism, a very modern phenomenon, is the result of limiting the self to rational intelligence and perceptions of only the 'external world'.

The Western church must take some responsibility for creating modern atheism. By exercising its social power to try to repress scientific, rational truth in the case of people such as Copernicus, Galileo and Darwin, it confused mystical knowing with rational, observant knowing. In the process, it discredited its own mystical knowledge and helped set up secular, rational intelligence as the new orthodoxy.

God was not ever, and will not ever, be known by the scientific way of knowing. God is known mystically by seeds sown in self and world. We know this. It is why religion has not disappeared in secular society, merely been removed from the public marketplace into private closets.

Intellectual atheism is modern, but practical atheism is as ancient as humanity. This is the kind of atheism practised by Patrick White before his slip-in-the-mud theophany. Practical atheism is living with such self-absorption that God is ignored—ignored spiritually and ignored morally. White says that, in his twenties, he was 'too well entrenched behind [his] own egotism and [his] father's allowance' to consider or embrace any big picture of self and world. He was thinking both of communism, a faith adopted by people he greatly respected, and God. He says: 'For many years I felt no need for a faith either dialectical or mystical, believing as I did in my own brash Godhead.'[12]

None of the great mystical maps debate the existence of God. They take for granted that we know. Nowhere, for example, in the Bible is there a discussion about God's existence. But there is deep probing about God's nature—especially, say, in the book of Job, about whether God is good and kind or evil and cruel.

Psalm 14 seems to be an exception. It says: 'Fools say in their hearts, "There is no God".' But 'fool' in this ancient biblical wisdom literature is not equivalent to the modern rationalist's 'illogical' or 'stupid'. Nor is 'heart' the equivalent of 'mind'. The vocabulary is of a richer, more complex picture of the self than the simple mind–body dualism of secular rationalism. The imagined atheism is practical, not intellectual, atheism.

'Fool', in this wisdom saying, has more the sense in modern English of 'unwise', 'lacking life sense', 'arrogantly egotistical'. 'Heart' is the self in totality: it includes mind, will, psyche, body and spirit. Thus, the writer's meaning is not that it is illogical to deny God, as if God's existence was a matter for debate. Rather, the meaning is that practical denial of God results in perverse, unwise and destructive living.

Apart from Jesus himself, the Bible knows no clearer affirmation of the intuitive, mystical knowledge of God than the writings of St Paul. Like the Psalmist, he, too, was concerned about the destructive, living-death outcomes of practical atheism. Of practical atheists, he says:

> . . . what can be known about God is plain to them, because God has shown it to them. Ever since the creation of the world, his eternal power and divine nature, invisible though they are, have been understood and seen through the things he has made. So they are without excuse.[13]

No language is able to capture our deepest apprehensions and feelings. We try to give them voice through more overt and concrete metaphors than are available in ordinary language. Faced with the shallowness of 'I love you' to express the depth of what I feel for my small daughter, I would say something like, 'I love you so much I could gobble you all up'. Or trying to 'say' what we 'feel' in the despair of depression, we use a phrase such as 'I'm in a dark cloud'. If words fail to express our own self-understanding, how much more difficult it is to speak in words about God, the great 'I'?

✠ *Mysterium tremendum et fascinans*

In his famous book *The Idea of the Holy*, Rudolph Otto chose a Latin phrase *mysterium tremendum et fascinans* to try to express our fundamental apprehension of God. God, for Otto, is the huge mystery which, seductively, attracts and fascinates us. 'Holy' is the word the biblical, spiritual map-makers choose as the most apposite to express what God is.

Not surprisingly, it is a teasingly difficult word to make sense of. In part, it means 'separateness', 'otherness'. Otto sought to capture this sense of 'holy' by saying that God is the 'Wholly Other'. God is unique. Nothing else is like God. God is singular. God is transcendent.

Awe is the faculty by which we apprehend God as the great and fascinating mystery, the great 'I' from which all things come and by which they are. It is not uncommon to experience awe of the Wholly Other through nature. The sky, mountains, the ocean are all so awesome before our mortal bodies that experiencing them evokes the awe of their source and author, too. Music, painting, architecture and poetry are vehicles of human expression able to induce awe of God.

Even thinking—say, pondering the question, 'Why is there something and not nothing?'—may evoke it. Or it may come in the unexpectedly ordinary, such as slipping in the mud onto your back with rain pouring on your face. The holy is apprehended only by awe—the awe of God and the awareness of our own comparative nothingness in the face of God.

If someone said, 'I don't understand what you mean by this awe of the Wholly Other who is holy', then I would not continue with explanatory words. Words can no more express actual experience of the holy than words can express our experience of a sunset or of sexual orgasm. I would recommend to such a person a period of total silence, two or three days at minimum, preferably by the sea or in the country. No talk, no radio, no television, just silence. For centuries, the followers of Christ's religion have sought through silent retreat the renewal of the power of the holy in their lives when it has been trivialised by business and the mundane.

'Holy' has a moral connotation, too. Holy is direct apprehension of the good, the *summum bonum*, goodness-in-itself, which is God. My first experience of the holy in this sense was as the seven-year-old who caused injury to the feet of the boy on the opposing gang at infants school. As I said, I felt remorse at what I had done to the boy. But I also felt I had violated a great truth, a right order of things. Conscience is the faculty through which we mystically and intuitively apprehend God as the supreme good, as the holy.

Rational intelligence has always failed to create a system of ethics based on reason alone because the good is apprehended directly by conscience, not by reason. Reason's role is to clarify conscience, to clear it of cultural, interfering static, and to weigh up alternative moral actions in the complex world of human behaviour where so often no black or white alternative exists, but a .whiter grey is the only good attainable.

When someone threatens to smash a chair over our head, or to do something even worse, we know there is objective good, even if we cannot say how or why we know. But apprehension of the Holy One through conscience speaks to us not only of right, but also of our sin. It mirrors to us our ridiculous egoism, pride and arrogance— the source of all sin. As Patrick White says to his cousin, Peggy Garland: 'I am not good— I only know what good is.'[14]

To tell my small daughter 'I want to gobble you all up' is a bizarre image to express love. Literally interpreted, it sounds more cannibalistic than affectionate. In order to express their experience of the holiness of God, biblical mystics, too, employ bizarre imagery. A classic example is Isaiah's temple vision of the Holy One:

In the year that King Uzziah died, I saw the Lord sitting on a throne, high and lofty; and the hem of his robe filled the temple. Seraphs were in attendance above him, each had six wings: with two they covered their faces, and with two they covered their feet, and with two they flew. And one called to another and said:

'Holy, holy, holy is the Lord of Hosts:
the whole earth is full of his glory.'

The pivots on the thresholds shook at the voices of those who called, and the house was filled with smoke. And I said: 'Woe is me! I am lost, for I am a man of unclean lips, and I live among a people of unclean lips, yet my eyes have seen the King, the Lord of hosts!'

Then one of the seraphs flew to me, holding a live coal that had been taken from the altar with a pair of tongs. The seraph touched my mouth with it and said: 'Now that this has touched your lips, your guilt has departed and your sin is blotted out.' Then I heard the voice of the Lord saying, 'Whom shall I send, and who will go for us?' And I said, 'Here am I; send me!'[15]

This vision of the holy contains all the usual elements of the experience of God as the Wholly Other—awe, a humbling feeling, pangs of conscience, unworthiness. Its expression in word and image is fantastic. Yet Isaiah dates its happening to an event in the ordinary, everyday world of ancient Israel. Isaiah's vision occurred, he says, 'in the year that King Uzziah died'. Like all biblical mystics, prophets and seers, Isaiah is an inner-worldly, not an other-worldly, mystic. What he sees is intended to be part of ordinary, everyday life, not an escape from it—the transcendent in the midst.

Isaiah experiences grace at the conclusion of his holy vision. The Holy overwhelms him with his own insignificance and unworthiness, but also empowers him to live and act. This sense of grace and empowerment is always associated with what God is as holy. In modern terms, God is like a big-amp, high-voltage electric current—dangerous in potential but, with proper response, empowering and life-giving.

After his vision, Isaiah embarked on his spiritual career as a prophet in Israel—not so much a foreteller of the future, the way 'prophet' is used in ordinary language today, but as a person who calls others to holiness: a person who calls them to worship and serve the great 'I', the Wholly Other in the midst of life in the waking world of family, work and society.

Colin Wilson complains that mystical experiences are not easily put into words. And that is true. But 'words' for Wilson mean abstract prose. Isaiah and the other biblical mystics scoff at such a limited view by their willingness to stretch language in order to speak of what they have 'seen'. To appreciate their 'seeing', we must learn to mature our appreciation of language in much the same way our palates mature to appreciate good wine, cheese or oysters.

But if God, the *mysterium tremendum et fascinans*, is the supreme good, then why is there so much pain and suffering in the created world? And how do we grow beyond awe and unworthiness to the fulfilment of that Beatific Vision which Aldous Huxley first thought he saw under the influence of mescalin?

PART B:

FROM NAIVETY TO INNOCENCE

5.

Integrating the negative
The journey from No to Yes

P ATRICK WHITE DECLINED OUR INVITATION TO SPEAK AT the Eremos meeting, explaining his self-imposed limitation to speak publicly only about nuclear disarmament. This issue troubled him so much that, uncharacteristically, he took advantage of his standing as a Nobel Prizewinner to promote it.

Signing himself, 'Patrick White, Nobel Prize Literature 1973', he wrote in May 1984 an open letter to the US President, Ronald Reagan. It was a somewhat pompous, 'philosopher–king' style letter, which read in part:

> Money is the poison which infects and destroys all advanced societies. The money which dazzles those who manufacture armaments, deluded scientists and politicians. Humility could be the antidote, such as I remember in the soft voices, soft palms of the pullman car attendants, old black washerwomen, farmers, characters I spoke with along the road when I was a feckless youth doing the United States.
>
> But there is a greater humility than that which simple souls are born with: the humility which evolves after sophisticated intellects have wrestled with their passions, self-hatred and despair in their search for truth.[1]

If it made any sense to him at all, a letter such as this was unlikely to dent the political shell of a pragmatic, populist president like Reagan. For those with some knowledge of Patrick White's character, it does not gel to see him posing as a humility expert. To be fair, humility is a comparative matter and White may have been contemplating how much less humble he might have been apart from his sufferings.

✠ The difficulty of integrating the negative

White's own sufferings are typical of the introspective, self-analysing, intuitive seer and thinker. They are not the sufferings common to most people— of poverty, financial struggle, physical pain, war, boredom, estranged relationships and the death of loved ones. White's sufferings were concentrated in his self-doubt, the contradictions of his own nature, the purpose and meaning of his life. Without them, probably, he would have been even more the monster he came to see himself as in old age.

At sixty-nine, he described himself this way:

> I am this black, bubbling pool. I am also this leaf rustling in the early light on the upper terrace of our garden. In the eyes of God, the Eye, or whatever supernatural power, I am probably pretty average crap, which will in time help fertilise the earth. The books I have spent years writing will be burnt in some universal, or perhaps only national, holocaust. That is what I think tonight; no doubt I shall see differently in the morning, and as differently on every other morning I am fated to live through.[2]

What is of interest here, and in his letter to Reagan, is White's experience of suffering as somehow positively transforming— in his case, making him humble— though it is better to say 'more humble than otherwise he might have been'. For in truth, he did not have the insight to see that the black washerwomen of his youthful American travels were not humble, but humbled.

In 1973, I became friends for a time with a Jewish-Hungarian woman of my own age whose family had fled communist oppression during the Hungarian uprising of 1956. They lost everything— their home, their culture, their money— and were 'nothing', just refugees until accepted into Australia as immigrants. We met as sociology students while I was chaplain at the University of New South Wales.

One day, while we were musing about the meaning of life over a cup of coffee after a morning lecture, she burst out with an accusation I have never forgotten. She said: 'You Australians don't really understand anything because you haven't suffered enough.'

Her sufferings were more palpable than Patrick White's, yet she, too, was saying they were positively transformative. In fact, she was going further. She was saying that true understanding derives from suffering.

Briefly, we discussed what she meant. She explained that she was no masochist. She was not advocating that we should seek suffering in order to gain understanding. Rather, she was saying if we ignore, block, suppress or repress the actual suffering in our lives, then we fail to be what we can be; we become shallow. And that is how she saw most Australians.

Her view parallelled my own experience as a priest dealing with sufferers. But I had always let myself be too sentimental to admit it. What I invariably got from the sick and distressed was not, 'What meaning is there in this for me?', but 'Why is God letting this happen to me?' This was from people who, one supposed, when life's seas were calm and the sun was shining *never* expostulated, 'God, why are you so good to me?'

Sufferers do not need lectures about the possibility of suffering being positively transformative. They need love and comfort. To tell them 'God has a purpose in this for you' is emotionally and spiritually insensitive. And considering the breadth, height and depth of human suffering throughout history, it seems equally outrageous to entertain the notion that eventually, somehow, all suffering will undergo positive transformation.

But what seems most outrageous, almost obscene, is St Augustine's interpretation of human suffering. According to him, all suffering is God's judgment upon humanity for the sin of our primal parents, Adam and Eve. In other words, the human race gets what it deserves. It is all *our* fault. This view has captured the mind of the Western church— one we will come back to in the next chapter.

✵ Carl Jung's integration of the negative

Like my Jewish-Hungarian friend, Carl Jung viewed suffering as necessary for human understanding and growth. Such a notion is, of course, quite foreign to the mindset of secular rational intelligence where reason alone is life's teacher. Jung always thought of himself as a traditional, mainstream Christian.

For Jung, the unconscious relates us to a psychic and spiritual world equal, as it were, in infinity to the 'external world' which consciousness seeks to understand through science. In other words, Jung sees human beings as creatures at the intersection of two worlds. One is known to the conscious self, the other to the unconscious self.

Psychology, for Jung, is the means by which we understand the unconscious. Below the unconscious, he says, is the fundamental reality, the eternal world of God. He says that we only acquire a true or total self when our conscious self and our unconscious self are brought together in mutual understanding. The self which then exists is the self which can relate healthily to God. Religion, with its myths, dogmas, theologies and symbols, speaks directly to the unconscious. Christian teachings, symbols and forms of worship are the most psychically health giving of all spiritualities. But for Jung it is a major error to interpret them as primarily relating to the conscious self. To do this is to create an absurd and magical literalism.

Like Freud, Jung saw his psychology as a science, a science of the psyche. Clearly, this is as untrue in his as in Freud's case. There is simply no way of verifying all that either of them claim to be true. Thomas Aquinas probably got the reason for this right when he said the higher we ascend the chain of being, the less precise, but the more important, is our knowledge. Thus our understanding of human nature, of the mind, of the psyche— our understanding of God and the spiritual— will always be less precise than our understanding of the objects of the 'external world'. Compared with physics and biology, theology, spirituality and psychology will always seem vaguer, yet in their long-term significance for us as people will be more important. But as with Freud, Jung is an artist of the psyche and his theories are pregnant with insight.

Let me bring Jung's grand theorising down to earth by letting it show the psychic dimension of my 'St George's light' theophany.

According to Jung, there are two main stages of human life. In the first half of life, we are taken up with establishing ourselves:

marrying, having children, nurturing a family, fulfilling social obligations, gaining skills in our work, establishing a business, making a career. Jung developed his psychology prior to the modern feminist movement, so he saw men in the first half of life more taken up with career and acquiring intellectual skills, while women sacrificed these things for the sake of their children. If much has changed— and that is an open question— then (some) women now are even more pressured than men to establish themselves in the first half of life, juggling home and career.

By middle life, which Jung thought was somewhere around forty, whether we have succeeded or failed in establishing ourselves, we begin to question what we have become— our meaning and purpose in life.

This was exactly the position in which I found myself at thirty-eight years of age. I had married, succeeded academically in several fields, been a reasonable success as a clergyman, become a published author. Then came the depression of unknown source: a period of intense mental and spiritual suffering. And, eventually, a profound questioning of all that I had become and where I was meant to go.

Jung says that if we are to find new purpose in the second half of life, we need to incorporate into consciousness those parts of the self we ruthlessly repressed in the first half of life. For women who have focussed on children and family in life's first half, this will mean the cultivation of intellect and seeking a place in the public social world. For men, it will mean shifting their attention from intellect and work to intimacy, relationships and leisure.

For modern women who have juggled family–nurture and career, the ruthless repression has been very powerful. In the

second half of life, they may need to seek new kinds of relationships and new ways of caring for themselves, not only for others.

Jung also thinks that it is necessary in the second half of life
to develop our spiritual lives which we repress in the busyness of
the first half. This includes the necessity to prepare ourselves for
eventual death.

For me, the end of ruthless repression that began in middle
life was allowing the intuitive and mystical parts of my consciousness to emerge. Though they were always there as the deepest
part of my being, they had been savagely repressed by my
intellectual and rational development in life's first half. In practical
terms, change meant spending more time alone, going on retreats,
acting on intuition, being not just a preacher and teacher but a
liturgist able to interpret Christ's religion in symbol and ritual.

If we fail to seek integration, if we fail to develop our
spirituality in the second half of life, Jung thinks we will suffer,
even go mad. Failure will produce transformation, but it will be
negative transformation— psychic or psychosomatic illness of some
kind or other.

Psychic and spiritual growth is a painful process. We know
this and seek to avoid the pain by ignoring, blocking, suppressing
and repressing it. We build a dam wall against the river of our
sufferings. But the waters swell up behind the wall. We put more
and more effort into building it higher and stronger. Inevitably,
there comes a time when cracks begin to appear in the wall,
uncontrollable side channels flow round it, a flood comes over
the top or, worst of all, the whole wall collapses.

Cracks may take the form of some kind of substance addic-
tion; side channels may appear as seemingly causeless neurosis or
psychosomatic illness; the flood over the top as depression; the

collapsed wall a full-blown psychosis. The pain that results from ignoring, blocking, suppressing or repressing our pain is a worse pain—worse, because it is a mystery. We do not understand its cause because we have so successfully blocked it out in the first place. It is like a phantom, a demon in the soul.

✠ Jane: coping with extreme psychic and spiritual pain

Jane was a blocker and a represser. She came to see me after taking an overdose. A chef, Jane has moved frequently from job to job. We first met at a party given by a mutual friend. Jane was above average intelligence, but not academically inclined.

What impressed me about her was the sensitivity of her 'crap antenna'. She could sense cant, shallowness, game playing and hypocrisy the proverbial mile off. She was twenty-two, so I wondered how such a young person acquired so much insight into herself and others. This mystery was solved when she informed me that she had been in therapy with a psychiatrist for six years. She did not explain why. It was a casual meeting, a party conversation. But it apparently gave her the confidence to make an appointment to see me later, after she had taken an overdose.

Jane told me the critical parts of her life story, the sources of the pain that rendered her suicidal. When she was just six and the boy who lived next-door fourteen, he began systematically abusing her sexually. This continued until she was twelve. She 'solved' the problem by avoiding any situation of encounter which he could exploit. She told no-one about it. He had threatened her with violence against any disclosure.

Performing badly at school, at age sixteen Jane became deeply depressed and suicidal. She had no idea why she felt this way.

Unbelievably to her now, when she first consulted the psychiatrist she had no conscious memory of the sexual abuse, the pain was so deeply repressed. It surfaced as 'uncaused' depression and suicidal thoughts. Working with the psychiatrist, the painful memories surfaced.

Jane's memory is not false. She has made contact with other victims of the same boy and he himself has actually admitted his abuse. She has not taken criminal action against him because she does not think she could survive the humiliation of a court hearing.

Jane knew all this when she came to see me. She had such profound insight. Then why the overdose? Why was she still so depressed and suicidal?

As we talked, I came to realise that her anger was still dammed up. Without a court hearing, without a criminal conviction and public humiliation, the perpetrator went free while the victim suffered. 'Why should he strut around and be respected when underneath he's such a shit?' she complained.

We talked about going to the police, but she had been through that option, over and over again, both with the psychiatrist and a sex abuse counsellor. She was adamant: 'I couldn't bear the humiliation of being cross-examined in court about what he did to me,' she said.

I checked to make sure she was not blaming herself for the abuse, victimising the victim. She had been through that issue over and over, too. It was not the problem. The psychiatrist had covered it with her. Our appointment ended, but Jane said she would like to see me again. 'Telephone when you're ready,' I said, feeling a hopeless failure and wondering why she wanted to see such an unhelpful person again.

When I saw Jane a few weeks later, she brought with her a notebook in which she had been writing. She referred to it in a casual, offhand way, but I guessed there was something in it she wanted me to read. I said, 'Would you like me to hear what you've been writing about?' 'If you want to,' she replied in a doesn't matter tone. What I then read was a short story of just three pages in Jane's handwriting. It took the form of a fairy tale. The wicked monster in the story said to one of Jane's fictional children: 'This is my body which is given for you.'

I instantly recognised these as the words of Jesus when he shared the bread at the institution of the eucharist. I say them every Sunday as part of the thanksgiving prayer at the altar. I made no comment until I had finished reading the whole story. In my obtuseness, I had not really seen the full import of the monster's words. However, I sought carefully to frame the right question: 'Jane, are you aware that the words of your monster include words spoken by Jesus?' I asked.

'Yes,' she replied.

'Why? What's the significance?' I enquired.

Her chin against her chest, she said, 'They were the words he used when he anally raped me.'

I am not a professional counsellor, but a spiritual guide. My work is to lead people to God and to walk with them on their spiritual journey, so my response was personal rather than professional. I exploded— exploded in utter anger against her abuser. I used expletives of the kind not to be written here. The word 'blasphemy', a word I seldom use, came onto my tongue several times. Blasphemy against God and blasphemy against Jane was what I felt he'd committed. My rage finally calming down, I said: 'So the bastard screwed you up spiritually as well as mentally and sexually!'

We talked on and on that day and subsequently, too. Two matters emerged as critical. First, what to do about all Jane's still suppressed anger. This is what was surfacing as her continued depression and suicidal feelings. Cleverly, Jane devised a plan whereby she could publicly expose her abuser amongst his family, friends and workmates. Only her abuser would know it was she who had done it, as only he would recognise the details of her disclosure. His family, friends and workmates, she recognised, might not believe the anonymous information they would receive, but she would be satisfied by the doubts it would sow.

'At least they will wonder why someone was angry enough to say these things,' she argued. I did not see her plan as seeking revenge but justice. She said that my explosive anger had helped her admit the gnawing depths of her own anger.

Jane possessed a near-perfect understanding of the causes of her pain. Yet she continued to be depressed and suicidal. Her suppressed anger was not sufficient to explain this. She was brilliant at her work, but totally unstable, moving from job to job every few months. 'I can't seem to change,' she would say. 'I know it all, but it makes no difference.'

With spiritual abuse so enmeshed with sexual abuse, I hesitated to speak with her about God. Yet I could see that this was the second critical issue. 'What image must she have of God?' I thought. 'This is my body' does not represent to her Christ's self-sacrifice of love, but an abusive, aggressive sexuality. So I said to Jane, 'Knowing the causes of our pain is usually just the first stage of getting it all together. We then need a power beyond ourselves to help us change—the power of love.'

'Are you talking about God?' she asked. 'I hate God.'

My guess about her image of God had proved correct, so I said: 'Forget God. Let's call it "It". Do know that "It" loves you?' I shouldn't have been, but I was surprised when she said 'Yes'.

For some weeks, we never spoke the word 'God', but always 'It'. Jane is slowly getting her life together since she began to open herself to the love of 'It', which, recently, she has begun to call 'God'. In a later chapter, we will come back to the power of God as love.

Those parts of the self which we ignore, block, suppress or repress always strike back at us in some way or other. They are not seeking revenge, but healing. The pain of the psychic, psychosomatic or spiritual 'strikeback' is as purposeful as the pain experienced bodily when we touch something hot or sharp. It is a danger signal, a warning of damage and destruction. The symptoms are not the true illness. Our symptoms are just the pointers to our true pain. We need to attend to them.

✠ Robert: coping with psychic pain

Jane's pain was both psychic and spiritual. This is a common combination, though the horrific causes of it in Jane's case are, thankfully, not so common. Robert's avoided pain was only psychic.

Robert was thirty-three when I first met him. There were two parts of his own behaviour which were compulsive, mysterious and repugnant to him. He frequently went on drunken binges. And, whether drunk or sober, he was frequently violent towards his wife and small children.

Robert had served as a conscript in the Vietnam War. Not only had he failed to face the pain of all he had seen and done during that war, he had failed to face the pain of returning home to a country that did not want to know about Vietnam veterans. He had been conscripted to serve his country, had participated in the horror of war, but returned not to the welcome of a hero, but to the ostracism of a pariah.

Now, as I came to know him, Robert was on the verge of destructive alcoholism, his wife about to leave him. Only by bringing all his repressed pain to the surface, including sharing it with his wife, was Robert able to start getting himself and his life together again.

✠ Coping with spiritual pain

Sometimes, our avoided pain is not psychic at all, but spiritual. Spiritual pain may arise from suppression or by simple neglect of the spiritual content of the unconscious.

Jung was acquainted with the damage Christian missionaries caused tribal peoples in Africa in the nineteenth century: a damage of multiple causes—'overdetermined', as the psychologists say. Missionaries were insensitive to traditional tribal religion, not bothering to understand it, dismissing all of it as primitive idolatry, not open even to the possibility that it was God's way of preparing spiritual soil for more fertile seed. They sought to impose Western culture on tribal culture, unaware how much they themselves had Westernised the Eastern religion of Jesus. Jung says:

> If you break up a tribe, they lose their religious ideas, the treasure of their old tradition, and they feel out of form completely. They lose their *raison d'être*, they grow helpless. That medicine man, with tears in his eyes, said 'We have no dreams any more.' 'Since when?' 'Oh, since the British are in the country.'[3]

Jung thought religious experience quite normal and that our psychic health, especially in the second half of life, depended on its expression as much as on the expression of our instincts. He was troubled that the secular West would lose its own *raison d'être*, its Christ-dream, and be prey to dangerous 'isms' and 'ologies' if it repressed religion and spirituality. Jung says:

> . . . generally speaking, religious experience is something we are fairly well acquainted with. We have the history of religions; we have innumerable texts which inform us about the forms of religious experience. So we know it is a universal phenomenon and, if it is absent, then we are confronted with an abnormal case.
>
> If somebody should say, 'I don't know what a religious experience is', then I say something is lacking, because the whole world has at times religious experience, and you must have lost it somewhere if you don't know what it is. You are not in a normal frame of mind. There is some trouble. When that is the case, we know that some other type of psychological function is exaggerated through the admixture of the energy which should normally be in a religious experience.[4]

Secular society probably has a number of Jung's 'exaggerated psychological functions' diverting, wrongly, its spiritual energy. A major one, which had not previously occurred to me, became obvious in 1988 when Dom Bede Griffith visited our home in Canberra. Bede Griffith, who has since died, was a Roman Catholic priest who lived most of his life in India where he founded the first Christian Ashram.

He, and some of the Indian friends accompanying him, were astonished and amazed at the attention secular Australians pay to their physical selves— health, dress, grooming— whilst appearing almost heedless of their spiritual well-being. They gasped at Australian devotion to gyms, work-outs, jogging, sports, exercise bikes, backyard pools, diets, vitamins, health foods, tonics, lotions, creams, powders and deodorants whilst spiritually seeming poorer than an Indian beggar.

In India, I had gasped equally at the reverse: spiritual devotion amidst material poverty. Their shock and 'tut tuts' were exactly the same as mine in India. It was a startling revelation to see an affluent secular society through the spiritual eyes of India. Ever since, I have experienced secular spiritual poverty as tangible.

Angus' story epitomises the pain which results from ignoring the spiritual self. Angus came to my chaplain's office at the University of New South Wales in late October, just before final examinations commenced. I had never met or seen him before. He was in an exceedingly agitated state, barely able to speak coherently. He told me he was in the last year of his medical degree. I assumed worry about his forthcoming finals explained his het-up state.

Not exactly jumping in with both feet but being strongly directive, I began to counsel him about exam nerves. This went on for a few minutes. Instead of the calming effect I hoped for, I noticed his agitation increasing. Finally, he burst out saying:

> Look, if I was worried about my exams, I'd have gone to see a counsellor. I'm not worried about them. I always get distinctions or high distinctions and I'll graduate with first class honours. I came to see you because you are a clergyman. I'm nervous because I've never spoken to a clergyman before. I want to know what it's all about, what's the point of it all? *That's* what I'm here for. Please do your job.

All this was said very politely, but was I put in my place. And rightly so! As I said in an earlier chapter, an easy trap for clergy to fall into in a secular society is the counselling trap. We turn ourselves into amateur psychologists when we should be spiritual guides. Angus' rebuke has remained in my mind to this day.

Angus told me there had been no religion in his life at all. Whilst not anti-religious, his family never talked about God, about life's purpose, about death—never read spiritual books or went to church. They were good people, he said, but their horizon did not extend beyond family, work, a few friends, the house, the garden, boating and golf. 'Is that it?' Angus asked. 'You eat, sleep, screw, work, play, eat . . . is that it?'

It's a long story, and a story that goes on because I still see Angus every now and then, but that day Angus took his first step on the journey home. He began to become a full person. His spiritual self emerged from the womb of the unconscious. He did, by the way, graduate with first class honours.

With courage, adequate care and spiritual guidance, almost all our psychic and spiritual pain can be transformed positively into growth of person and spirit, even the pain of knowing that you are dying.

✠ Mary: coping with death

I had never met Mary. She was fifty-three when I called on her at her daughter's request. Mary had agreed to the visit, so an appointment was arranged. A few weeks before my visit, Mary's doctor told her she had inoperable liver cancer. Medical opinion could not predict how long she had to live—maybe a few weeks, maybe several months. My first visit passed with not much more than polite, trivial conversation and a cup of tea. I enquired whether she would like me to come again. She said she would and a time was fixed for the following week.

During my second visit, Mary, who had seemed quite well the previous week, lay on top of her bed— not ill enough to be in bed, but not well enough to be up, either. Each of us knew the other was aware she had only a short time to live. I sensed she did not want to pussyfoot about, so I said, 'Mary, what are you feeling about what the doctor told you?'

Thus began a deep psychical and spiritual journey that was to last through weekly sessions together until she died about five months later. Oscillating back and forth between them, Mary went through the various stages of dying as described by psychologists— denial, anger, bargaining, depression, acceptance etc. Spiritually, we started off with Mary saying:

> I've believed in God all my life, but I've never done anything much about it. I've hardly ever been to church or said my prayers. I feel guilty about turning to God now when I need him. I've ignored God so much that I feel ashamed to ask for help.

This was a very big hurdle to straddle. We first read together the story in St Luke's Gospel about the two criminals crucified with Jesus:

> One of the criminals who were hanged there kept deriding him and saying, 'Are you not the Messiah? Save yourself and us.' But the other rebuked him, saying, 'Do you not fear God, since you are under the same sentence of condemnation? And we indeed have been condemned justly, for we are getting what we deserve for our deeds, but this

man has done nothing wrong.' Then he said, 'Jesus, remember me when you come into your kingdom.' He replied, 'Truly I tell you, today you will be with me in paradise.'[5]

I said, 'Mary, Luke clearly interprets Jesus to say God's love is unconditional, that God is always waiting to accept us.' But it was many weeks before Mary overcame her shame barrier and accepted this for herself. Slowly, she felt able to pray and meditate. She began reading the Gospels and, on the few occasions when she was well enough, came to church and received the sacrament.

Mary had been divorced for many years. The marriage break-up was a bitter one and she blamed her husband for it entirely. Her second daughter took her father's side and became estranged from Mary, too. These matters came into our sessions indirectly, from Mary's dreams.

From the start, I invited Mary to tell me about her dreams. I am Freudian enough to believe that our dreams expose what is going on at the deeper levels of our lives. (Incidentally, by taking dreams seriously as possible sources of meaning, Freud, at this point, was closer to the seers, prophets and apostles of the Bible than to secular rationalists.)

I never try to interpret the meaning of another person's dreams. I only ask questions to help them make their own interpretation. At first, Mary found it hard. She had never paid attention to her dreams before. But as the weeks passed, she looked forward eagerly to this part of our time together. Like most dreams, the images, the situations, the happenings were eerie, exotic, fantastical. Her interpretations kept throwing up two painful issues: her former husband and her estranged daughter.

We began talking openly about both. She told me the story of her unhappy marriage and its eventual collapse. She had kept her feelings at bay for years, dammed behind a great wall of bitterness she systematically constructed. This wall came tumbling down as Mary revisited in detail the arguments, the scenes, the drunken brawls. For the first time, she admitted to herself the part she had played in them. It was not just his fault anymore; she took responsibility, too. She even saw her daughter's estrangement in a new light. Mary had virtually insisted the girls take sides. And they had taken sides, one on Mary's and one on her former husband's. She now accepted her own part in the estrangement from her second daughter.

I knew her husband had remarried. But after she had dealt with her own sins, I asked her to consider making contact with her husband and second daughter, seeking reconciliation. She took up this suggestion. I did not witness the reunion, but graciously her former husband came, with his new wife, to visit Mary and so did her estranged daughter. What I did witness was the joy in her eyes and the relief from tension in her face afterwards.

About a month before she died, Mary said to me, 'I bless God for my cancer; it has been a great gift'. I kissed her and thought of the words of the litany we pray on Good Friday—'From dying suddenly and unprepared, Good Lord, deliver us'.

My last visit to Mary was the day before she died. She was very ill, the morphine barely keeping pain at a tolerable level. She was pleased to see me, but obviously too weak to make much conversation. But she was anxious to tell of a dream she had had the previous night. She said that in the dream an ambulance came to collect her. A stretcher was slipped underneath her as she lay supine upon her bed. Then she was lifted from the bed and placed on the floor beside it. As the ambulance men lifted her down, she said she watched her own body change into the body of Christ. There was no interpretation of the dream that day; we both knew what it meant. We smiled at each other and kissed goodbye. She died the next day.

✠ Abuse of the dying

Probably since the dawn of history, no culture has psychically and spiritually abused the dying so thoroughly as modern secular Western culture. This is the consequence, first, of rational intelligence dealing only with the external world, in this case with the physical body and with bodily death. And the consequence, second, of a closet religion which is too shallow and private to cope with death's sufferings and finality.

Medically, rational intelligence is very successful, developing knowledge and techniques able to prolong the life of the terminally ill. But because it has no public knowledge of anything except bodily life, secular rational intelligence intervenes excessively to extend physical life when the outcome is nothing much but prolonged, futile suffering. Where the natural course of a disease would lead to a relatively quick death with minimum physical suffering, excessive intervention leads to long, humiliating, depressing and agonising death.

Sometimes, the medical profession is blamed. This is unfair. The profession is only doing what secular society demands. Very often God is blamed. This, too, is unfair. Sufferings which derive from excessive and ultimately futile medical intervention are caused by the one-dimensional vision of secular rational intelligence. And whilst a huge proportion of economic wealth continues to be spent on physical health, almost nothing is spent on the psychic and spiritual health of the dying.

Closet religion cannot provide the depth of knowledge necessary to care spiritually for the dying. An Australian secular-intellectual, whose young adult daughter died from the prolonged effects of a brain tumour, was recently reported as saying at her funeral on his own and his wife's behalf:

> [We] . . . have been through a terrible eighteen months watching our lovely young daughter drift, day by day, hour by hour, out of reach. That has been tough enough to bear, but it would have been unendurable if we had held the belief that there was someone up there who personally knew of these events and had been heartless enough to make them part of his divine plan, or if we had believed there was someone who might have intervened on our behalf to prevent such a terrible outcome, but had wilfully failed to do so.[6]

In these words, one can feel the inner pain of a grieving father and empathise as much as is possible for those of us on the outside. But the image of the rejected God, the 'someone up there', is the magical, adolescent image of closet religion or fundamentalism.

Secular rational intelligence knows almost nothing about death or God except to repress thought about both. To ordinary, everyday rational consciousness, death is the ultimate negative. Excessive medical intervention which seeks to prolong physical life at the cost of increased suffering is part of this repression: a vain attempt to negate the negative.

The possibility that, somehow, even this ultimate negative might undergo positive transformation is absurd. Thus, louder and louder calls are made not for the palliative care of the dying, not for adequate psychic and spiritual care, but for euthanasia. To secular consciousness, the notion of a 'good death', which is the literal meaning of 'euthanasia', is not the healing of psyche and spirit as the body disintegrates, but assisted suicide.

✠ St Francis of Assisi: Welcome, Sister Death

St Francis of Assisi is one of the most integrated human beings who ever lived. Renowned for his care of the poor and afflicted, delighting in the natural world, friend of the animal kingdom, full of the joy of life, he is known as 'the little Christ'. Francis' joy and delight in life are expressed in his famous hymn/poem, *Laudato sia Dio mio Signore*, which is still sung regularly in churches today, more than seven centuries after it was written. It starts:

> All creatures of our God and King,
> lift up your voice and with us sing
> alleluia, alleluia!
> Thou burning sun with golden beam,
> Thou silver moon with softer gleam,
> O praise him, O praise him,
> alleluia, alleluia, alleluia!

Each verse continues with the same structure, inviting all of nature and all human beings to praise the creator in celebration of life. Wind, water, stars, fire, flowers, fruit, mother earth herself are invited to praise God with alleluias. Then comes to modern secular ears the shock of the penultimate verse:

> And thou, most kind and gentle death,
> waiting to hush our latest breath,

O praise him, alleluia!
Thou leadest home the child of God,
and Christ our Lord the way hath trod;
O praise him, O praise him,
    alleluia, alleluia, alleluia.

In his book on St Francis, subtitled 'A Model for Human Liberation', the Brazilian Catholic theologian Leonardo Boff says:

> One of the most difficult traumas to resolve for the human psyche and for the attainment of freedom is exactly that of death. It seems like the supreme negation of life. It frustrates the most fundamental driving force of the life system, according to Freud, the true dynamic nucleus of each being—that is, desire. Desire is radically the desire for life without any negation, desire for an always real freedom and for limitless happiness . . . Tradition calls the drive for life Eros . . .
>
> A sign of human and religious maturity is to integrate the trauma of death in the context of life. Then death is dethroned from its status as Lord of life and ultimate reality. Eros triumphs over Thanatos [death] and desire wins the game. But there is a price to pay for this immortality: the acceptance of the mortality of life. The acceptance of death.[7]

Francis of Assisi died in 1226. At the end, he could not retain food, was vomiting blood and, according to Celano's biography: 'The doctors were frightened and the brothers marvelled that his spirit could live in a body already so destroyed, because his flesh had been consumed and there only remained the skin on his bones.'[8]

He was moved from Siena to Assisi and taken to the bishop's house. A doctor attended him, reporting that nothing could be done. Francis called the members of his order around him to sing a canticle together. He added the verse:

Praised may you be my Lord, for Sister
Bodily Death, whom no one escapes.
Woe to those who die in mortal sin!
Blessed be those who fulfil the will
of God, because the second death will
do them no harm.

Boff says such an attitude to death caused outrage even in the
thirteenth century:

Such joviality was a scandal to common sense. The general
of the order, Brother Elias, seeing the uselessness of the
situation, said to Francis: 'Father, I am very glad that you
feel so much joy; but I fear that in the city, where they take
you for a saint, it would be scandalous for them to see that
you are not preparing properly for a good death.'

'Do not be troubled,' Francis answered him. 'With all my
sufferings, I feel so close to God that I can do nothing but
sing.'[9]

As he sensed his final hour approaching, Francis asked to be
moved again: to the chapel of Our Lady of the Angels of the
Portiuncula where his ministry had begun. He asked the brothers
to sing, joining them as best he could. Boff says:

Then he asked the brothers to place him naked on the
earthen floor, to 'fight nakedly with the naked one'. It
was a gesture that rose from his innermost being. More
than an extreme identification with the naked Crucified
Lord, it expressed the profound desire of the psyche for
communion with Mother Earth; we come naked from her
and we return to her naked.

Like an immense uterus, she thrusts us from her embracing
womb, representing thusly and in the language of symbols

the total integration of humanity with God, the great and good Mother.[10]

Integrating the negative means not to ignore, block, suppress or repress the actual pain in our lives, but to confront it, seeking its positive transformation. Not to confront our actual pain, paradoxically but truly, is to suffer worse pain.

Mary and St Francis integrated death, the negative of negatives. This I call 'the healing through death'. Nothing in today's secular world is more thoroughly ignored than the healing through death.

✠ Healing through death

If God is good and God is love, then death cannot be the end of life, but a metamorphosis. It is impossible to accept that God contrived elaborately to bring the universe to consciousness in human beings, only to snuff us out into nothing again.

But if God is good and God is love, then the cruel injustices of life also demand an arena of redress: a world where Caligula, Napoleon, Hitler, Stalin, Idi Amin, Pol Pot and all their lesser-likes finally face the music. A world where the raped and murdered child, the young conscript lying body-blasted dead on the battlefield and all victims are soothed and healed of their agonies and nightmares. We know that this is required. But is it so?

A secular rational consciousness will say 'no'. But where is its doubt? Whence this certitude? It must not be permitted to repress its doubt. No-one 'knows' what actually lies beyond death. By repressing the knowledge of death, by prudishly censoring death as obscene, secular consciousness ignores the possibility that death is a mere shadow, a sleep through which we are intended to pass to the beatific vision of God. Through its repression, secular consciousness infers to itself that death is nothingness, whilst hiding in the spiritual closet the secret hope that it may be a doorway to greater life.

Even if we see death as possible nothingness, repression of the knowledge of death robs us of life. To face death, admitting we do not know what comes after, is to live more fully than to live delusively, without doubt, in the certitude of death as nothingness.

In Shakespeare's *Hamlet*, the doubt of death is a question of life. And the doubt is enlightening. Hamlet's psyche, sick with morbid sexual imaginings (possibly incestuous Oedipal desire), murderous and vengeful thoughts, asks what it is to be human and mortal:

> What a piece of work is a man, how noble in reason, how infinite in faculties, in form and moving, how express and admirable in action, how like an angel in apprehension, how like a god: the beauty of the world; the paragon of animals; and yet to me, what is this quintessence of dust?[11]

Shakespeare rightly poses together the questions of life, of meaning and of values with the question of death. Death's doubt is instructive. To live in its face is to live deeply. Hamlet's most famous speech is more explicit still:

> To be or not to be, that is the question,
> Whether 'tis nobler in the mind to suffer
> The slings and arrows of outrageous fortune,
> Or to take arms against a sea of troubles,
> And by opposing, end them. To die, to sleep—

No more, and by a sleep to say we end
The heart-ache, and the thousand natural shocks
That flesh is heir to; 'tis a consummation
Devoutly to be wished to die to sleep!
To sleep, perchance to dream—ay there's the rub—
For in that sleep of death what dreams may come,
When we have shuffled off this mortal coil
Must give us pause . . .
But that the dread of something after death,
The undiscovered country, from whose bourn
No traveller returns, puzzles the will,
And makes us rather bear those ills we have,
Than fly to others that we know not of?
Thus conscience does make cowards of us all . . .[12]

In the next chapter, we will come back to consider Hamlet's musing that there may be a 'dread of something after death', especially for people such as Hitler or Stalin, but first let us think about the greater life beyond death.

I studied for my divinity degree in the early 1960s. In that era, the world of rational intelligence was awash with empiricism. Empiricism is the view that nothing is true unless it can be tested and verified by the experience of our physical senses.

The early 1960s was also an era of super-confidence in science. Science was going to explain everything and solve all human problems— or so it was believed. In this period, science itself was thought to be the simple practice of empiricism. Scientists were supposed just to look up telescopes, down microscopes and in test-tubes in order to find the truth passively waiting there to be discovered.

As you know, I studied at Moore, an Anglican College in the

grounds of the University of Sydney. That Moore is in those university grounds and is Anglican deepened even further the sea of empiricism in which I undertook my initial theological study. The school of philosophy at the university was dominantly empirical. So, too, was British philosophy in the motherland of Anglican Christianity. Not surprisingly, theology sought to respond to empiricism by proving that it itself was empirical, too.

As I have said before, the religion of Christ is an Eastern, historical, inner-worldly, mystical religion. By trying to prove it had empirical credentials, theology in this era concentrated on the historical stratum. So I was taught in the lecture room, and via the books of the day, that the whole of Christianity depended on historical proof, especially proof that Jesus Christ rose from the dead. It is not a caricature to summarise the view espoused in this way:

> The resurrection of Jesus from the dead is an empirically provable historical fact. Any rational person can see this. If, having seen it, they still reject Christianity, then it is because they are moral rebels against God. If it wasn't possible to prove Christ's resurrection empirically and historically, then it would be stupid for anyone to be a Christian: it would all be nothing but a fairytale.

Any confidence I ever had in this apparently logical and simple approach—and it wasn't much even at the tender age of nineteen—was shattered forever when I tried it out one day on a Sydney University philosopher.

'Oh,' he said, 'let me accept, for argument's sake, that you have indeed proved as an empirical, historical fact that Jesus

Christ rose from the dead. So what? An interesting and highly unusual phenomenon of the first century!'

The resurrection of Jesus is first and foremost an event that has to be interpreted— that has meaning as we understand it against the totality of Christ's life and death and future glory.

✠ Making sense of life and death: the big picture

Today, everyone knows that no big picture of life can be proved by the experience of the senses, by empiricism. Not evolution, not secularism, not materialism, not atheism, not anarchism, not Christ's religion— not anything. But we do all live by a big picture. Our big picture might be nothing more than 'This is all there is, so live' or 'Everything is relative', but we all have one. Human beings, it seems, cannot be human without forming some kind of big picture of life to live and die by. But the only real test of the truth of any big picture is the sense it makes of everything we do actually know and experience.

I do not believe that it is possible to prove empirically as an undoubted historical fact that Jesus rose from the dead. Even if you could, then, as the Sydney philosopher said, 'So what?' All that can reasonably be established is that the first followers of Jesus sincerely believed that he appeared to them alive after he had been crucified and entombed— and that they were so confident about his continuing life they were prepared to put their own lives on the line in order to continue his radical teachings and announce him as the clue to the meaning of life.

Something I do not merely believe but know is that integration of the negative is not only possible, but also that it is physically, psychically and spiritually healthy and life-giving.

I know that false selves must be put to death painfully for more real and whole selves to rise. I agree with my Jewish-Hungarian friend that we know most via our sufferings. All this makes a very good 'fit' with the big picture of Jesus as the suffering–dying–rising God incarnate. The bare empirical fact of a human being rising from the dead is remarkable, but is truly a 'so what?' More important is the issue of *who* is said to have risen from death to life.

One Easter morning, I tried to explain this to a large, rural congregation by starting my sermon saying:

> Adolph Hitler is risen from the dead.
> Adolph Hitler is risen from the dead.

I used a booming voice and then kept quiet. I had intended the silence to last for a couple of minutes so people could think about why I had made such a solemn, totally outrageous pronouncement. But immediate stirrings and whispers in the congregation, and the facial expression on some of the farmers who looked much bigger and stronger than me, induced me to proceed hastily.

But before I explain what I went on to say in that sermon, it is important to understand what the first followers of Christ's religion meant by claiming he had risen.

They did not have the view, popularised by modern fundamentalism, that Jesus hopped out of the tomb on the Sunday morning after the Friday crucifixion, walked around on earth for forty days and then, like a spaceship, took off in a cloud to heaven. Any careful reading of the Gospels or St Paul's letters will show quickly that the Jesus who appeared after his death appeared from heaven (God's world, not to be confused with the sky). Resurrection and ascension to heaven were part of the one event.

Unfortunately, history has contributed to the crude picture by celebrating the resurrection and the ascension on two separate days in its spiritual calendar. Further confusion has arisen from dividing the Gospel of Luke and the Acts of the Apostles into two separate biblical books, rather than seeing them as a single work.

At the end of Luke's Gospel, there is a story of an appearance by the risen Jesus to a gathering of his disciples in Jerusalem, after which the author says he was carried up to heaven. At the beginning of Acts, Jesus appears again. This is followed by a very dramatic story of another ascension into a cloud. (Clouds in the Bible, fittingly, are symbols of God and heaven.) The intention of the second, dramatic ascension story is to mark finality. It is saying, 'This is the end of Jesus' appearances; now God will be present to the followers of Christ through his Spirit'.

Putting aside the modern crudities, too often aided and abetted by Hollywood movies, what the first-century followers of Christ understood by the resurrection was appearances of Jesus alive from heaven. The resurrection and ascension were parts of the one happening. Jesus rose from the dead to God.

Coming back to my Easter Day sermon, what I next said was:

> If Adolph Hitler— or for that matter, Jezebel, Julius Caesar or Stalin— made definite appearances alive from heaven to their followers, then it would tend to confirm in our minds a different solution to life's jigsaw puzzle than the one taught and lived by Jesus.

It is harsh to say it, but a resurrection appearance by Adolph Hitler or Joseph Stalin would tend to confirm that Bertrand Russell had got the nature of ultimate reality pretty right. Russell, of course, defiantly refused to live by the impersonal, destructive, amoral nature of his God. Unfortunately, this was not the case with Hitler or Stalin.

For Jesus Christ, ultimate reality was personal, infinitely caring, purposeful and promising final human fulfilment. His disciples interpreted his appearances alive from heaven as God's confirmation of Jesus' teaching. For them, the one who appeared was the same one who said not a sparrow falls from the sky without touching the heart of God, the same one who gave himself in love to lepers and prostitutes, the same one who rejected the sword and accepted the self-sacrifice of the cross.

No-one can prove empirically the resurrection–ascension of Jesus. It can only be accepted as making most sense of all we do know and experience. It is unlikely to make sense to anyone who has not, in Patrick White's words, 'wrestled with their passions, self-hatred and despair in their search for the truth'. To those for whom it does make sense, the ultimate negative is integrated.

6.

Thinking the unthinkable

The spiritual journey from naivety to innocence

I OFTEN SAY, 'IF IT WASN'T FOR JESUS CHRIST, I WOULD believe in God, but I wouldn't trust God'. Gerry's story will help to explain what I mean.

Gerry was a journalist with a Sydney television station. He lived in Paddington when I was the rector of the Anglican church there. I first met Gerry when he turned up for church one Sunday morning. He was in his mid-thirties.

After church, we talked over a cup of coffee. Gerry told me that he had been quite religious until he was eighteen. He had attended Sunday school, had been confirmed, worshipped regularly at church and said his prayers most nights. He said his image of God was the picture of a benign parent presiding over a beautiful world where all was well— in his words, 'A God of blue skies, sunsets, birds and flowers'.

When Gerry was eighteen, his sixteen-year-old sister, with whom he was close, was killed in a car accident. Blue skies turned grey for Gerry that day. This disaster neither fitted with his image of life nor of God. He stopped going to church and ceased believing in the benign parent who presided over all.

'Why then,' I asked, 'have you come to church today?'

His reply intrigued me. 'I feel pretty silly about saying this. It should have been obvious. You see, I catch the bus to work every day. I have been travelling on it for years. The bus route takes me past quite a few churches. This week it hit me for the first time that the symbol on every church is the cross. So I started thinking about it. Why the cross? I realised the cross is about suffering and that God must have something to do with suffering. So I came to church to try to find out what it is.'

Whilst awaiting execution in a Gestapo prison for his complicity in the plot to assassinate Hitler, Dietrich Bonhoeffer, son of the Professor of Psychiatry at Berlin University and Germany's most able young theologian, said, 'Only a suffering God will do'.

Gerry had begun to understand this profound insight.

✠ The legacy of childhood

I am mostly thankful that I did not grow up in a religious family. I say 'mostly', because I can see the problems either way. Growing up in a religious family can leave you with an infantile or spiritually damaging image of God. Growing up in a religiously indifferent family can leave you in a spiritual desert and make you prey to spiritual nonsense or religious fantasy. In my case, I was fortunate to get involved in a mainstream church, not a fringe group or cult.

But the mainstream can also give you problems. I remember a conversation I had with my father when I was about thirty and he had stopped saying he was an atheist. He said, 'How come you got caught up in that ratbaggery about alcohol and refused to eat your mother's sherry trifle?' I replied, 'Well, Dad, it could have been worse. You gave me nothing spiritually, just a vacuum. I had no litmus paper to test with.' By this time, we were good adult friends. His reply, 'Fair enough, son', indicated to me his acceptance of the criticism.

Gerry's family situation was the opposite. They and his church had created an image of God in him that was childish. The first time it encountered harsh, adult reality it dissolved as useless. But Gerry was fortunate, too. At least his childish image was benign. I know many adults whose family-created image of God is perverse. Most of them struggle between atheism in their heads and quiet despair in their hearts. They have terrible pain dealing with the question of God at all.

The worst instance I know is Arthur's. Every morning from the onset of puberty, Arthur had to present himself for masturbation inspection. If his father thought Arthur had dark rings under his eyes, he concluded that Arthur had masturbated during the night and gave him a thrashing.

I met Arthur when he was seventeen. He was a brilliant student and a belligerent atheist. Arthur was one of those atheists who delight in trumpeting their unbelief, especially to members of the clergy. He loved attending our church youth club to stir me. Sometimes, I would drive him home afterwards. It was late one night, sitting in the car outside his house, that he told me about the masturbation inspections.

Arthur was never going to find peace and purpose with a God we call 'our Father'. The last time I heard from him he was in his early forties. He has never been able to hold a job and suffers severe and apparently incurable psychic illness. He told me he was studying Eastern mysticism, the other-worldly kind which views God as impersonal. I cannot imagine that Arthur will ever find peace with God until he can picture God being thrashed for supposed masturbation, too. For Arthur, only a suffering God will do.

✠ Jesus and the problem of the unforgivable sin

The Jesus portrayed in the Gospels taught and practised universal love. He scandalised the religious authorities of his day by valuing as persons of worth and engaging socially those whom the authorities condemned as scum and feral. He told them God loved them, he loved them himself, and he offered them forgiveness of their sins. But according to the Gospels there is one sin Jesus held to be unforgivable: the sin against the Holy Spirit.

> Truly I tell you, people will be forgiven for their sins and whatever blasphemies they utter; but whoever blasphemes against the Holy Spirit can never have forgiveness, but is guilty of an eternal sin.[1]

It has always been difficult to know the intended meaning of this saying. The image of a God who is total love but who refuses to forgive a particular sin has created real angst for many people. Interpretation of the saying is not made easier by the fact that it is given more than one context in the different accounts of Jesus' life.

Through the ages, most scholars have taken it to mean that continuing and *persistent* rejection of God cannot be forgiven by God. After all, how is God able to forgive those who do not wish to be forgiven? Surely, only by a force which would not be love. Most clergy counsel those whose consciences are troubled with Jesus' words by explaining that any worry about having committed the sin is itself a sign of not committing it.

✠ Carl Jung and his childhood legacy

Carl Jung was one who worried about the unforgivable sin. Jung grew up in a very religious family. His father and two of his uncles were Swiss clergy. Consequently, he had to do battle with many family images of God in order to reach a mature understanding of his own. When he was eighty-three, Jung gave a long interview on BBC television, part of which went:

What sort of religious upbringing did your father give you?
Oh, we were Swiss Reformed.
And did he make you attend church regularly?
Oh, well, that was quite natural. Everybody went to church on Sunday.
And did you believe in God?
Oh, yes.
Do you now believe in God?
Now? [Pause.] Difficult to answer. I know. I don't need to believe. I *know*.[2]

Jung came to this certitude only through much suffering, especially by doing battle with his family's limited image of God.

This battle had its turning point when Jung was just twelve years old. Later in adult life, Jung would incorporate insight gained from the battle into his psychological theory, especially into the process he called 'individuation'. He describes the innocuous start to his twelve-year-old experience this way:

I came out of school at noon and went to the cathedral square [in Basel]. The sky was gloriously blue, the day one of radiant sunshine. The roof of the cathedral glittered, the sun sparkling from the new, brightly glazed tiles. I was overwhelmed by the beauty of the sight and thought: 'The

world is beautiful and God made all this and sits above it,
far away in the blue sky on a golden throne and . . .'3

He stops mid-sentence, for at this point another kind of
thought intruded itself into Jung's consciousness, a thought in
utter and lewd contrast to his perfect image of the summer's day,
the lovely cathedral and God's golden throne above.

For some days after, he continued to repress this thought. He
wondered if letting it come to consciousness might be to commit
the unforgivable sin. It disturbed him greatly:

> On my walk home, I tried to think of all sorts of other
> things, but I found my thoughts returning again and again
> to the beautiful cathedral I loved so much and to God sitting
> on the throne— and then my thoughts would fly off again
> as if they had received a powerful electrical shock. I kept
> repeating to myself: 'Don't think of it, just don't think of
> it.'4

As Jung describes it, this struggle went on for three days and
through sleepless nights. His mother became anxious about him,
but he refused to tell her what was upsetting him. He says he
knew he had to face it alone.

On the third night, he awoke from a restless sleep and his
thoughts turned again to the cathedral and to God. As he wrestled
to keep the forbidden image at bay, he mused on the biblical
story of Adam and Eve. He concluded that God must have
intended them to sin. 'They could not have done it if God had
not placed in them the possibility of doing it,' he thought. From
this, he concluded that his own spiritual courage was being tested
and he decided to permit the suppressed image of the summer's
day to come to full consciousness:

I gathered all my courage, as though I were about to leap forthwith into hell-fire, and let the thought come. I saw before me the cathedral, the blue sky. God sits on his golden throne, high above the world—and from under the throne an enormous turd falls upon the sparkling new roof, shatters it and breaks the walls of the cathedral asunder.[5]

What Jung says he then experienced was unutterable bliss and the miracle of grace. He became a 'knower', not a mere believer. Ever thereafter, he felt that he knew inwardly the truth his father only believed and preached outwardly. Jung says:

A great many things I had not previously understood became clear to me. That was what my father had not understood, I thought; he had failed to experience the will of God, had opposed it for the best of reasons and out of deepest faith. And that was why he had never experienced the miracle of grace which heals all and makes all comprehensible.[6]

Jung felt he had experienced the 'dark side' of God. This, he believes, is what God wants us to do. Instead of repressing our negative feelings about God, instead of suppressing our anger at God, Jung says we must *challenge* God—wrestle with God, as Jacob did with his mysterious nocturnal visitor. So long as we dance politely around a God sitting on his throne above his beautiful cathedral, we will, according to Jung, know little of God. Even at twelve, Jung had learnt the shallowness of whining about such a God or feeling rejected by 'someone-up-there' when life goes wrong. And especially, he had learnt the shallowness of a pale and compliant acceptance of that 'someone'. He says:

Why did God befoul his cathedral? That, for me, was a terrible thought. But then came the dim understanding that

God could be something terrible. I had experienced a dark and terrible secret.[7]

Jung's experience changed forever his image of God and left him totally dissatisfied with the formal, respectful belief of the Christianity of his family:

> The experience also had the effect of increasing my sense of inferiority. I am a devil or a swine, I thought; I am infinitely depraved. But then I began searching through the New Testament and read, with a certain satisfaction, about the Pharisee and the publican, and that reprobates are the chosen ones. It made a lasting impression on me that the unjust steward was praised and that Peter, the waverer, was appointed the rock upon which the church was built . . .
>
> In my mother's family, there were six parsons and on my father's side not only was my father a parson, but two of my uncles, also. Thus, I heard many religious conversations, theological discussions and sermons. Whenever I listened to them, I had the feeling: 'Yes, yes, that is all very well. But what about the secret? The secret is also the secret of grace. None of you wants to know anything about that. You don't know that God wants to force me to do wrong, that he forces me to think abominations in order to experience his grace.'[8]

Leaving aside for the moment the question of whether or not you or I might agree with his conclusion, I feel it is worth looking at the contrast set up between Jung's views and the more traditional view which has been largely shaped by Augustine. Jung's strong expression that God 'forces' him to do wrong in order to experience God's grace is a shock to all those with an Augustinian image of God.

✠ Augustine's view of suffering

As mentioned briefly in the last chapter, Augustine taught that as a human race we deserve all that we suffer. It is God's punishment upon our sin. Augustine explained the existence of evil as the mere absence of the good. All the evils of life, for him, are the result of human sin, of human rejection of God and of the good.

Jung, on the other hand, has also thought about the Adam and Eve story and concluded that God intended humanity to sin and suffer. He held that God, too, not just human beings, is responsible for sin and suffering.

Augustine and those who follow him are unable to explain why innocent inhabitants of pure paradise, Adam and Eve in the Garden of Eden, would ever have had the vaguest inclination to do wrong in the first place. And if they were not entirely innocent, the twelve-year-old Jung mused, then God must have actively placed the possibility of doing wrong in their nature— just as God, Jung believed, had placed it in him.

We must not imagine that Jung or Augustine were thinking about a literal, historical Adam and Eve. The story is not intended to be read that way. Augustine, for example, mostly interpreted the Old Testament stories as spiritual allegories. Today, we expect theology to be taught abstractly, the way philosophy or psychological theory is taught. But Hebrew theology in the Bible is usually taught by stories.

The Adam and Eve tale is a story which wrestles with such issues as the origin of evil, the source of sin and suffering, relationships between men and women, and the relationship between us and God. It is better to read it as a mini-Shakespearean play than as the introduction to a modern textbook, say, on ancient history or anthropology. But it is a story with the same truthful profundity as a Shakespearean play, never to be dismissed lightly as a childish yarn.

How did Jung view his own spirituality? He always saw himself in the mainstream of Christ's religion, although he doesn't always fit easily into that. On the other hand, however, it is easy but quite inaccurate to take some of his writings, which are voluminous, out of context and charge him with some superstition or other. Most commonly, the charge has been that Jung was 'gnostic'— or, in modern parlance, 'New Age'. Jung would certainly reject this charge. He knew a lot about Gnosticism and about the roots of modern New Age beliefs, but he always saw himself within the Christian mainstream.

For Western Christianity, so powerfully shaped by Augustine's image of God, it is not mainstream to say that God 'forces' us to do wrong in order that we may experience God's grace. Augustine's view, that all suffering is the result of human sin, has so thoroughly dominated Western Christianity that it has come to be equated with the teaching of the Bible itself.

Augustine's genius was as a systematic thinker. But his explanation of evil, sin and suffering does not capture the essence of Jesus' image of God as loving and good, but rather suggests an image of an overbearing, self-righteous Victorian father, given to playing favourites. Not only do we deserve what we get here on earth, according to Augustine, but, as a race, we all deserve eternal hell, too.

Augustine's only sense of God's love is that, having condemned humanity to the sufferings of this life and to eternal hell afterwards, God decides to rescue some of us by sending Christ. According to Augustine, those to be rescued have been especially chosen and the rest deliberately not chosen. He views the death of Christ as a sacrificial offering to atone for the sins of those whom God has predestined to save from universal and eternal condemnation.

Augustine's theology in a particular form will be familiar to all who have contact with contemporary Christian fundamentalism. Fundamentalists at times espouse such views as if they are the teaching of Jesus himself.

If I myself accepted Augustine's image of God, then what might I have said to journalist Gerry when he came back to church that Sunday morning seeking the meaning of the cross? Perhaps, something like this:

> Well, Gerry, your sister died in that accident because God has placed this world under universal condemnation for our sins. Not that your sister is any worse than the rest of us; no, it's just that God has put a plague on the whole world. It can strike any of us at any time.
>
> Your only hope is to repent of your sins, turn to God and place your faith in Christ's atoning sacrifice, trusting that you are one of those chosen to be saved from the hell to come. I'm sorry that your sister had not given her life to Christ in this way. I am not the judge, God is, but she is probably among the great mass who are damned eternally.
>
> But, Gerry, God is now giving you the opportunity to be saved. All you need to do is to repent, confess your sins and throw yourself upon the love of God by putting your faith in Christ and what he did for you by dying on the cross.

If Augustine's view of God were accurate—I don't believe it is!—then, regardless of the consequences that some might envisage, I would reject such a God as vehemently as Bertrand Russell rejected his 'God' of Impersonal Matter. If Russell's 'God' is uncaring and amoral, Augustine's 'God' is uncaring and immoral.

Where I do agree with Augustine, however, is that we are all sinners— in the sense that we all break our *own* moral standards, let alone Christ's golden rule that we must love others just as we love ourselves. Therefore, it makes sense that we need God's forgiveness to free us from sin and guilt.

✠ Tim and his childhood legacy

As a young undergraduate at Sydney University, I had a friend who brought this home to me tellingly. Tim grew up in a family with an Augustinian image of God. When I met him, he was an ardent and very self-honest atheist. As he grappled with his life, he commented one day:

> You know, I do not doubt the objectivity of morality. I know good and evil are 'there' just as up and down are 'there'. I accept that moral values are not just invented by me or by society. I also know that I do wrong as well as right.
>
> This leaves me with a big problem. I'm painted into a corner. How do I get rid of the guilt when I do wrong? I can't just forgive myself, because I didn't invent the moral good I've sinned against.

I remember that I said nothing, but just listened. What I thought was: 'Tim, one day you are going to get a bigger picture of God than the one you got from your family. Then, you'll know what to do about your guilt.'

As a twelve-year-old, Jung wrestled with God. It was wrestling, not believing, that made him a knower. He discovered that God was full of grace, a grace his father taught and believed but did not know. His discovery came from grappling with what he called 'the dark side of God'. This is something the Bible itself does.

✠ Job and his struggle with God

The Bible's Job would not explain God and suffering to Gerry in the way I imagined a good Augustinian might. Job would batter at God's door demanding an explanation for the unfairness of Gerry's sister's untimely death.

The Book of Job was written some time around five to seven centuries before the birth of Jesus Christ. At the outset, it describes Job as 'blameless and upright, one who feared God and turned away from evil'.

There are six main characters in the story: God, Satan, Job and Job's three friends— Eliphaz, Bildad and Zophar. The theology and spirituality is Eastern, conveyed by story and drama, not by Western rational abstraction.

Satan is not an opponent of God, as he will become in later biblical books (influenced, probably, by Persian thought), but part of the heavenly council. Satan's role in the story is like that of a prosecutor in a modern court of law. God praises Job to Satan. But Satan says that Job is such a fine fellow only because life has been so good to him:

> You have blessed the work of his hands and his possessions have increased in the land. But stretch out your hand, now, and touch all that he has and he will curse you to your face.[9]

God accedes to Satan's request to put Job's character to the test. Satan brings calamity upon Job. He loses all his wealth and all his children are killed. In deep distress, Job, nevertheless, remains pious and philosophical when he hears of his terrible misfortune:

> Then Job arose, tore his robe, shaved his head, and fell on
> the ground and worshipped. He said, 'Naked I came from
> my mother's womb and naked shall I return there; the Lord
> gave and the Lord has taken away; blessed be the name of
> the Lord.' In all this, Job did not sin or charge God with
> any wrong-doing.[10]

In the heavenly council, God and Satan converse again about
Job. God praises Job for his spiritual integrity despite the effects
of Satan's cruel test. Satan replies that Job will curse God if Job's
physical person itself is subject to pain and suffering. Satan says:

> Skin for skin! All that people have they will give to save
> their lives. But stretch out your hand now and touch his
> bone and his flesh, and he will curse you to your face.[11]

Here, Satan's voice speaks profoundly. It is the sufferings of the
flesh, of the futile pain of a cancer for which there is no cure, of the
rape and sexual torture of women, of Hitler's 'medical experiments'
on Jews and gypsies, that cause us to cry out in protest to God or
to reject God.

God gives Satan permission to put Job to this test. Job is
afflicted with loathsome sores from the sole of his foot to the
crown of his head. His wife, a minor character in the drama,
intervenes:

> Then his wife said to him, 'Do you still persist in your
> integrity? Curse God and die.' But he said to her, 'You speak
> as any foolish woman would speak. Shall we receive the good
> at the hand of God and not receive the bad?' In all this, Job
> did not sin with his lips.[12]

The narrator's words that Job 'did not sin with his lips' make us wonder, though, about what is going on in his heart and mind. Job's three friends arrive to console and comfort him. For seven days and seven nights, they just sit with him; no-one speaks. Job's suffering is too great for words. At the end of the seven days and seven nights, Job does not curse God, but he curses the day of his birth and longs for death:

> Let the day perish in which I was born,
> and the night that said,
> 'A man-child is conceived.'
> Let that day be darkness!
> May God above not seek it,
> or light shine on it . . .
> Why did I not die at birth,
> come forth from the womb
> and expire?
> Why were there knees to
> receive me,
> Or breasts for me to suck? . . .
> Or why was I not buried like
> a stillborn child,
> like an infant that never sees the light? . . .
> Why is light given to one who cannot
> see the way,
> whom God has fenced in?[13]

By not cursing God, but cursing the day of his birth, Job challenges and demands explanation from God. He does not reject God, but he demands God make sense to him of his suffering. This is not unlike the Gospels' report of Jesus' cry of dereliction from the cross which is both a prayer and a challenge:

My God, my God, why have you
forsaken me?[14]

Most of the Book of Job is taken up with verbal interchange
between Job and his three friends. His friends try to comfort him
with the kind of pious inanities still offered today to 'hope-less'
sufferers. The friends say such things as 'we deserve what we get',
'we are never innocent', 'we should submit and not ask questions', 'God has his own mysterious purposes'—and so on. But
Job persists with his challenge. How, he demands, can God be
just when there are unjust sufferings such as his in the world?

At the conclusion of the drama, God answers Job in two long
speeches. In these speeches, Job is treated to a parade of God's
great power and knowledge as the creator and sustainer of the
world. At the end of the first speech, God says to Job:

Shall a faultfinder contend with the Almighty?[15]

In the face of God's display of power and knowledge, Job
decides his only appropriate response is silence. Who is little Job
to challenge such greatness? He replies:

See, I am of small account;
what shall I answer you?
I lay my hand on my mouth.[16]

God's second speech catalogues the great land and sea animals
which God has created: animals which in size and strength dwarf
a human being like Job. Job, God says, cannot even control these
creatures and yet he throws down the gauntlet of moral challenge
to their creator. Who does Job think he is? God asks.

Job then submits himself to the almighty power of God. He says he now knows God as he has not previously known him. Experience has turned him from a mere believer to a knower:

> I know you can do all things,
> and that no purpose of yours can be
> thwarted . . .
> Therefore, I have uttered
> what I did not understand,
> things too wonderful for me,
> which I did not know . . .
> I had heard of you by the hearing
> of the ear,
> but now my eye sees you;
> therefore, I despise myself
> and repent in dust and ashes.[17]

After Carl Jung gathered courage and went through with his own challenge to God (and to his clergyman father), picturing the 'enormous turd' falling from heaven, he, too, felt small and unworthy. But Jung also experienced, as a consequence of the challenge, an overwhelming sense of God's grace. This happens to Job, too.

God restores Job's riches, he fathers new sons and daughters. But much more significantly, Job is charged by God to absolve his three friends of their sin. What is their sin? Their sin is all the shallow, pious answers they gave to Job in defending God against Job's challenge to God:

> . . . the Lord said to Eliphaz the Temonite: 'My wrath is kindled against you and against your two friends; for you have not spoken of me what is right, as my servant Job has. Now therefore take seven bulls and seven rams, and go to my servant Job, and offer up for yourselves a burnt offering;

and my servant Job shall pray for you, for I will accept his prayer not to deal with you according to your folly; for you have not spoken of me what is right, as my servant Job has done.'[18]

But 'God', the character in this drama, has not answered Job's challenge. God has only asserted his infinite knowledge, power and might, demanding Job's obeisance. Job buckles to this assertion of God's greatness but, in the process, becomes a seer, not a mere hearer— a knower, not a mere believer.

Job is commended for his challenge to God. His three friends, who sought to defend God, are know-nothings who must repent of their folly. They are like those theologians who have all the intellectual answers, but do not wrestle with God passionately and existentially, who talk about God but do not know God. They are also like Jung's father and his clergy colleagues.

The drama of Job might be left there, with no answer given to Job, just a bestowal of divine grace upon him after his challenge, wrestle and ultimate submission. Augustine's image of God, of course, would have us start with submission and forget the challenge. This is exactly what God condemns the three friends for.

Any careful reader of the Job story can see it cannot be left merely with submission and grace. Jung was aware of this.

The God in the story, 'God' the character, is not to be equated with God as such. Only a simplistic, literal reading of the Book of Job would interpret it this way. It is the *whole* story, every character as well as 'God', that seeks to penetrate and reveal the true God who will, of course, ever remain in essence a mystery. It is important to see this because, in a profound sense, 'God', the character, as Jung saw, comes off worse than Job.

Job submits not to some loving and tender explanation of why unbearable, unjust suffering is justified, but to an overweening display of might and authority. Little, finite, mortal Job is certainly inferior to 'God' in knowledge and power. But with his challenge to God's goodness, justice and love, it is little, finite, mortal Job who appears morally superior to 'God', the *dramatis persona* in the story. In part, 'God' comes across as a despot or tyrant.

Certainly, Job's moral superiority is tempered by 'God's' commendation of his challenge and by 'God's' condemnation of the three smarmily pious friends. But Job is not answered. His legitimate questions are not answered. He is just forced to submit.

Is there any answer to Job's challenge?

Shortly, I want to explore this question by looking at an understanding of God, sin and suffering in Eastern Christianity, an understanding quite different from the Western one inherited from Augustine. But first it is relevant here to tell you how I came to write this book.

✠ The journey from naivety to innocence

Bathurst, the city where I live, is about two hundred kilometres west of Sydney. The town boasts just one cinema which, for understandable reasons of profitability, tends to screen only popular, blockbuster movies. To see so-called art and foreign language films, we must take a seventy-kilometre car trip into the mountains towards Sydney to a small town, Mount Victoria.

If the weather is mild, after a session at the Mt Vic Fliks, we sit talking, eating and drinking at tables on the lawn of a local pub. In winter, we do the same inside the pub, by a huge open fire. Recently, a friend of a friend drove up from Sydney to join us for a 'film and feast' session. Discussion about the film led into conversation about the meaning of life.

We had the usual laugh about the black joke in *The Hitchhiker's Guide to the Galaxy*, where a super-computer gives the answer '42' to a question fed into it about life's meaning. I bantered that the computer's answer, in fact, was very knowing (I was born in 1942).

'Well,' said the Sydney visitor after the inevitable guffawing died away, 'what do you say is the meaning of life?' She fixed her gaze on me as much as to say, 'Shouldn't a bishop have a bit more to say than mere jestering about '42'?' I had not met her before and had forgotten that this woman, in her early forties, had been recently widowed.

What is the meaning of life? This is a question which, from what you have read so far, you will know is one I, too, have wrestled with for most of my adult life. A spiritual guide should indeed have something to say about it. Clergy are in the meaning business or they don't mean business. Our job, and a tough one it is at times, is to mine meaning in much the same way others mine opals or diamonds.

I answered entirely without thinking. It just 'came out'. What I said was such a surprise that I felt as if someone else had spoken it. Had I reflected, let myself think a while, I am sure I would have given a different answer. My reply was: 'The meaning of life is to journey from naivety to innocence.'

I was glad the pub lawn party did not want to discuss my answer. They kindly said they wanted to ponder it. I wanted to ponder it, too. I am not sure I had even begun to understand my own answer. And these ponderings are what led to this book and to whether there is an answer to Job's challenge or not.

7.

Massacre of the innocent

Only a suffering God will do

_____

IN THE EASTERN CHURCH, THERE IS AN INTERPRETATION of the Adam and Eve story which is quite different from the Western, Augustinian interpretation. It has never had the same systematic development as Augustine's theory, but it makes more sense of all that we know and experience.

This interpretation is older than Augustine's-fifth century view. It goes back to Irenaeus, who was Bishop of Lyons in the second century.

✠ Irenaeus' view of the path to human maturity

Whereas Augustine viewed the Adam and Eve legend as a story of the rebellion against God by innocent but non-naive adults, Irenaeus saw Adam and Eve as more like silly, immature children—naive rather than innocent. Thus for Irenaeus, we humans, spiritually as well as physically, are created as children. We are made in the divine image, and given freedom and responsibility, in order that we might grow into the kind of mature adults God intends us to be. In the words of Irenaeus himself:

For as it is certainly in the power of a mother to give strong food to her infant [but she does not do so], as the child is not yet able to receive more substantial nourishment; so also it was possible for God himself to have made man perfect from the first, but man could not receive this [perfection], being as yet an infant.[1]

Irenaeus views the sin of Adam and Eve, not as a damnable, adult revolt against God, but rather as an infantile rebellion to which God responds with compassion on account of their weakness and vulnerability. He says:

This, therefore, was the [object of the] long-suffering of God, that man, passing through all things, and acquiring the knowledge of moral discipline, then attaining to the resurrection from the dead, and learning from experience what is the source of his deliverance, may always live in a state of gratitude to the Lord, having obtained from him the gift of incorruptibility, that he might love him more; for 'he to whom more is forgiven loveth more'.[2]

Irenaeus explores the idea that God deliberately hides from us, that divine self-revelation is always intentionally ambiguous, so that we may have moral and personal freedom. In more modern parlance we might say, 'By grace, God has so created us and our universe that we are free to be atheists'. Not that Irenaeus would wish anyone to be an atheist, if indeed he ever thought in those terms, but he did see the hiddenness of God as a condition of human freedom. Perhaps a better picture of his idea is that of a parent holding back adult intervention to allow a child to learn from her/his mistakes.

For Irenaeus, it is necessary that the world contain a mixture of good and evil. Moral and spiritual growth can take place only when such a contrast exists:

For just as the tongue receives experience of sweet and bitter by means of tasting, and the eye discriminates between black and white by means of vision, and the ear recognises distinctions of sounds by hearing; so also does the mind, receiving through the experience of both the knowledge of what is good [and what is evil], become more tenacious of its preservation, by acting in obedience to God . . .[3]

If instead of giving Gerry the journalist an Augustinian explanation of the suffering experienced through his sister's tragic death, I was to give him an Irenaean one, then, perhaps, it would go something like this:

Gerry, your sister's death is a terrible tragedy. But God has made the world a place where such accidents can happen. Most suffering is caused by the sins human beings commit against each other; some is just built into the way things are. We are all going to die of something some time.

God hides from us by creating an ordered universe built on a foundation of randomness and chaos. A certain amount of freedom and randomness in the natural world is necessary in order that we might be personally and morally free. This world is like the world of a fairytale, a world of great wonder and beauty *and* a world of threatening monsters.

While ever we live in it, God wants us to grow: to grow as persons, morally and spiritually. The experience of suffering, and of dealing with our suffering, is part of the growth. Jesus Christ is the example *par excellence* of the adult maturity God intends for each human being. Jesus suffered. The cross is our continuing symbol of his sufferings. But the cross is now empty, bare—because he is risen to heaven.

Such an explanation still falls short of Gerry's own insight about crosses on churches— the insight that God has something directly to do with suffering through Jesus Christ's sufferings. To this, I will return shortly. But first, a summary of an important difference.

✠ Irenaeus and God's part in sin and suffering

The English philosopher John Hick puts the difference between Irenaeus' undeveloped view and Augustine's systematic theory this way:

> Instead of the doctrine that man was created finitely perfect and then incomprehensibly destroyed his own perfection and plunged into sin and misery, Irenaeus suggests that man was created as an imperfect, immature creature who was to undergo moral development and growth and finally be brought to the perfection intended for him by his Maker.
>
> Instead of the fall of Adam being presented, as in the Augustinian tradition, as an utterly malignant and catastrophic event, completely disrupting God's plan, Irenaeus pictures it as something that occurred in the childhood of the race, an understandable lapse due to weakness and immaturity rather than an adult crime full of malice and pregnant with perpetual guilt.
>
> And instead of the Augustinian view of life's trials as a divine punishment for Adam's sin, Irenaeus sees our world of mingled good and evil as a divinely appointed environment for man's development towards the perfection that represents the fulfilment of God's good purpose for him.[4]

Carl Jung believed that God 'forced' him to do wrong in order that he might discover God's grace. I find myself very uneasy with this view. It makes God less than a responsible human parent. A good parent may stand back and allow a child to do wrong, knowing that that is how the child will learn to discriminate between right and wrong, between the helpful and the harmful. But a good parent will not *force* a child to do wrong. Jung has overreacted to his parents' puerile image of God, which was, according to Jung, an image of fearful, correct belief without passion or engagement.

Irenaeus does not say that God forces us to do wrong. But he clearly implies that God knowingly creates us as conscious creatures whose immaturity will lead us to do wrong. In other words, unlike Augustine, Irenaeus implies that God bears responsibility with us for our sin and for our suffering, in that he created immature beings with that capability.

This was certainly Job's charge against God. And 'God', the character of the Job drama, both denies and accepts this charge. The charge is denied by 'God's' assertion of power and might, demanding Job's humble submission. The charge is accepted in that 'God' commends Job as a person of spiritual integrity and condemns his three pious, sycophantic friends. We might all experience something of Job's commendation if, instead of a cheap, intellectual denial of God or a pale spiritual submission to God, we took courage to pursue our anger, questions, doubts, despairs and negativities with passionate engagement of God.

✠ The massacre of innocents and the intuition of damnation

The question of sin and the question of meaning can never be entirely separated. What most raises our doubts about whether we can discover life's meaning in the eternal purposes of a

personal Creator, who is both good and loving, is the abominably
wicked cruelties human beings wreak on each other. Whether
we are thinking of Hitler's holocaust, Stalin's labour camps, the
American napalming of Vietnam, ethnic cleansing in the Balkans,
the massacre of innocents, the sexual abuse of Jane, or Arthur's
morning masturbation inspections, the question arises: 'Why does
God permit such atrocities?'

If we are truly honest with ourselves, we shall have to ask
why, too, God permits us to perform our own acts of sin and
cruelty against others.

The Irenaean answer is that the licence to perform such
wrongs is a condition of being persons, a condition of our
humanness as conscious, morally free agents. This makes good
sense to us ourselves if we are fairly ordinary, humdrum sinners.
It is reasonably easy, by analogy, to view God as the parent who
stands back to let us grow into spiritual and moral maturity by
working through issues about our faith, our doubts and our sins
and by learning from our mistakes. But it makes very little sense
of the horrific victimisation and abject cruelty of war, tyranny,
torture or even of what goes on behind the front door of some
seemingly polite and civilised family homes. Many of God's
children do not grow into the adult image of Jesus Christ, but
into monstrous, adult demons.

As an adult, I have done much worse things— mostly of a
spiritual, psychological and inter-personal kind— than when, as a
child, I put in the sand the broken glass which cut a boy's feet
to pieces. But I knew then that I deserved a fateful retribution.

Although Augustine's theory of God's wrath leads, with its
oversystematising, to an image of God as tyrannical and imperi-
ous, showing only a tad of compassion by granting mercy to a

chosen few, it does contain the essence of a deep truth. If monstrous, adult demons are never brought to account, then how can God be good?

Peter Berger, an American sociologist, explores this question in his book *A Rumour of Angels*. He examines experiences which all of us have— built-in theophanies— that transmit the reality of God to us. He calls these experiences, these rumours of angels, 'signals of transcendence'. He lists and explores quite a number of them. But one such signal, he says, is our in-built sense of the necessity of damnation. Berger says:

> This refers to experiences in which our sense of what is humanly permissible is so fundamentally outraged that the only adequate response to the offence as well as the offender seems to be a curse of supernatural dimensions.[5]

Berger has in mind the Nazi outrages. But he is aware that, historically, this is but one example of horrendous human evil. Thus he thinks, too, of the torture and murder of children and the innumerable massacres of the innocent stretching back to the dawn of human history. He says:

> There are certain deeds that cry out to heaven. These deeds are not only an outrage to our moral sense; they seem to violate a fundamental awareness of the constitution of our humanity. In this way, these deeds are not only evil, but monstrously evil.[6]

As one of the world's leading sociologists, Berger is well aware of the whole debate about the relativity of morality. This is exactly why he has chosen to focus on our sense of injustice, rather than justice, as the clearer 'signal of transcendence'. Anyone who doubts the intuitive and mystical reality of this signal within their own consciousness should view, or view again, Steven Spielberg's film of the Nazi holocaust, *Schindler's List*. Berger says of such horrors:

> These are deeds that demand not only condemnation, but damnation in the full religious meaning of the word—that is, the doer not only puts himself outside the community of men; he also separates himself in a final way from a moral order that transcends the human community, and thus invokes a retribution that is more than human . . .
>
> The massacre of the innocent (and, in a terrible way, all of history can be seen as this) raises the question of the justice and power of God. It also, however, suggests the necessity of hell—not so much as a confirmation of God's justice, but rather as a vindication of our own.[7]

If, in the case of monstrous human evil, the question of sin and the question of meaning cannot be separated, neither can they be separated in the case of ordinary human evil such as afflicts us all. We will come back later to the fate of the damned, but first we need to explore the connection between Christ's suffering and death and the love of God.

✠ Jesus' suffering and death and the love of God

As said in an earlier chapter, the image of Jesus Christ as God incarnate originally derived from reflection upon the actual experience of the life and teachings of Jesus. It was an image which grew, as it were, from earth to heaven, not from heaven to earth. This must not be overlooked. Otherwise the incarnation becomes just a dogma to be believed or disbelieved, on the authority of others. It loses its roots in experience and in reflection upon experience. But once the earth-to-heaven and the heaven-to-earth connection is made with experience, and not mere dogma, many other things begin to make sense— including hints of an answer to Job's challenge to God.

Less than half a generation after the events themselves, Jesus Christ's suffering and death were being seen as a means whereby human beings could receive God's love and the forgiveness of their sins.

Our current age of secular, rational intelligence is not much concerned about sin and forgiveness. Underneath its preoccupation with creating a secure, prosperous everyday life, its angst is more about meaninglessness and purposelessness than about sin and guilt. But as I have said, and hopefully demonstrated, in the case of monstrous evil, the question of sin and the question of meaning cannot be entirely separated.

In part, the relationship between meaning and sin has been obscured by the Western church's morbid obsession with sexual sin. This has made the word 'sin' a great turn off for a culture which has discovered the joy of human sexuality and which is itself compassionate and forgiving, not harsh and judgmental, about the complexities, trials, troubles and sins of human sexual relationships.

There is nothing in the Gospel stories about Jesus to suggest he shared the church's obsession with sexual sin— indeed, nothing to suggest he was otherwise than gentle with the sins of human weakness, including sexual weaknesses. But Jesus fiercely challenged the sins of power, the sins of economic, political and religious abuse. And it was the 'powers' who had him killed for troubling them.

Languishing in the Gestapo prison at Flossenburg, awaiting execution, Dietrich Bonhoeffer, the convinced pacifist who became convicted that his own head of state must be eliminated, wrote:

> Even the Bible can find room for the Song of Songs, and one could hardly have a more passionate and sexual love than is there portrayed . . . It is a good thing that that book is included in the Bible as a protest against those who believe Christianity stands for the restraint of passion (is there any example of such restraint anywhere in the Old Testament?).[8]

In the light of his experience in Nazi Germany and the kind of society he thought might follow the end of World War II, Bonhoeffer saw the pathetic weakness of a Christianity which grubs away at sins of human weakness whilst ignoring the sins of power. He wrote:

> . . . it must be said that man is certainly a sinner, but by no means mean or common. To put the matter in the most banal way, are Goethe or Napoleon sinners because they were not always faithful husbands? It is not the sins of weakness, but the sins of strength which matter here. It is not in the least necessary to spy out things. The Bible never does so . . .
>
> This is why I am so anxious that God should not be relegated to some lost secret place, but that we should frankly recognise that the world and men have come of age, that we should not speak ill of man in his worldliness, but confront him with God at his strongest point, that we should give up all our clerical subterfuges and our regarding of psychotherapy and existentialism as precursors of God.[9]

As a victim of Nazism's monstrous evil, Bonhoeffer, the brilliant young theologian, became aware of the awesome danger of neglecting adult humanity in its strength. One suspects that the Western church's continued fascination with sexual sin during the fifty years since Bonhoeffer wrote these words, and the subsequent secular revolt against the whole notion of sin, would alarm him even more. If confident adult men and women have little or no sense of their sins of strength then, as the atheist Ivan says in Dostoevsky's novel *The Brothers Karamazov*, 'everything is permissible'.

Granted that the Western obsession with sexual sin is a gross distortion of Christ's religion and granted that we are all sinners, then what is the connection between Christ's sufferings and death and God's love?

Popular Western understanding of Christ's suffering and death became distorted from the Middle Ages on. This distortion continues today—especially among fundamentalist Christians. The distortion has very little in common with the way the original followers of Christ's religion understood the meaning of his suffering and death. I slightly parody it here to bring out the simplistic nature of the conclusion:

We are all wicked sinners.

The awesome, almighty God is very angry with us, because of our sins.

Nice Jesus Christ loves us and gave up his life in self-sacrifice to bear the punishment we deserve for our sins.

Nice Jesus Christ has atoned for our sins and placated God's anger against us.

If we repent, confess our sins and ask for forgiveness, trusting in Jesus, then 'angry' God will forgive us on account of what 'nice' Jesus did for us.

This is not as much a parody as it might seem. When I joined my local Anglican church as a teenager, I heard an even cruder version than this one. I was told that God is like a judge in a criminal court. I was the defendant who stood guilty of crimes worthy of death and eternal hell. Any sin deserved this penalty, it was said, mine as much as Stalin's. But Jesus would come into the court and take my place, so the argument went, if I would let him.

I did not accept this crude argument even at seventeen. But at that age, I could not counter it with a deep explanation of the meaning of the death of Christ.

Even in maturity, Carl Jung took for granted that the 'angry God/nice Jesus' distortion was the definitive, mainstream Christian view. The distortion horrified him. He rejected it. But the way he rejected it did take him, at this point, away from the mainstream of Christ's religion. He came to view God not as good and loving, but as a *mixture* of both good and evil— though, if I understand him correctly, he thought God's 'good side' would eventually prevail over the 'bad side'. He felt that the 'angry God/nice Jesus' distortion demonstrated no real growth of spiritual insight from the story of Job's challenge to God to the incarnation of Christ.

Jung says:

Redemption or deliverance has several different aspects, the most important of which is the expiation wrought by Christ's sacrificial death for the misdemeanours of mankind. His blood cleanses us from the evil consequences of sin. He reconciles God with man and delivers him from the divine wrath, which hangs over him like doom, and from eternal damnation.

It is obvious that such ideas still picture God the Father

as the dangerous Yahweh (of Job) who has to be propitiated. The agonising death of his Son is supposed to give him satisfaction for an affront he has suffered and for this 'moral injury' he would be inclined to take a terrible vengeance.

Once more, we are appalled by the incongruous attitude of the world creator to his creatures, who to his chagrin never behave according to his expectations. It is as if someone started a bacterial culture which turned out to be a failure. He might curse his luck, but he would never seek the reason for the failure in the bacilli and want to punish them morally for it . . . Moreover, a bacteriologist might make a mistake in his choice of a culture medium, for he is only human. But God in his omniscience would never make mistakes if only he consulted with it.[10]

When I was a small child, my father was always inclined to deny my requests to visit friends, go to the cinema, have extra money to spend on a special outing. On the other hand, my mother was inclined to comply with my requests. But first, by virtue of the nature of their own relationship, she had to persuade my father. No doubt, there was something Oedipal about these transactions— mother giving in to the male child's requests, father refusing the male child, but relenting at the intercessions of his female partner.

As a result, I came to see my father as the stern, solemn figure in my life and my mother as the soft, easy-going one. This is how the 'angry God/nice Jesus' distortion divides God up.

The first-century biblical writers did no such thing. They did not picture God as Jung's bacteriologist. It is astonishing that someone of Jung's knowledge and mental capacity should accept this distortion and shows how deeply it has sunk into the Western mind.

Although it would take more than three centuries to formulate an agreed, satisfactory form of words to state how Jesus might be understood as both fully human and fully divine, the first-century biblical interpreters of Jesus already saw him that way. In story form (the virgin birth stories of Luke and Matthew) and in sophisticated Greek philosophical terms (the *logos*-made-flesh of John), they spoke of God incarnate in Jesus Christ. They saw the whole life of Jesus— his incarnation, teachings, sufferings, crucifixion, resurrection–ascension— as one continuous action of God. There was no wrathful 'father-God' and nice 'brother-Jesus' in their view. Thus, approximately two decades after the crucifixion, Paul was saying: 'God was *in Christ* reconciling the world to himself' (2 Corinthians 5: 19).

For Paul, what Christ does God does. There is no fracture. The 'angry God/nice Jesus' distortion derives from analogy with the medieval law courts and came to dominate the Western church through Anselm of Canterbury's book, *Cur Deus homo?* (*Why the God-man?*). Though to be fair, Anselm, who lived from 1055 to 1109, was never so crude in the way he theorised about Christ's death as are many today.

When the first-century biblical writers speak of God's purpose in Christ, including the meaning of his death, they do not think in terms of human law courts, but in cosmical, eternal, mystical terms. John, for example, uses the Greek philosophical term *logos* (translated into English as 'Word') to explain Jesus. In modern English, *logos* means something like 'meaning' or 'purpose'. John opens his Gospel by saying:

> In the beginning was the Word [Purpose] and the Word [Purpose] was with God and the Word [Purpose] was God.

He was in the beginning with God. All things came into being through him, and without him not one thing came into being . . . And the Word [Purpose] became flesh and lived among us, and we have seen his glory, the glory of a father's only son, full of grace and truth.

Here Jesus, the Word made flesh, is one with God. According to John, what Jesus is and does, God is and does. There is no 'angry God/nice Jesus' dichotemy.

For John, it is God's love for the created world that motivates God's incarnation in Jesus, as he says in chapter 3, verse 16:

For God so loved the world that he gave his only Son, so that everyone who believes into [*sic*] him may not perish, but may have eternal life.

Patrick White discovered in himself a complex, contradictory set of characters. But there was also, whatever we like to call it, a continuity of person, a self or soul that allowed there to be a Patrick White able to write about his complex and contradictory characters. We are all the same. It is in the very nature of human personhood for there to be both a self of continuity and an internal dialogue of characters. We are conscious and we are self-conscious beings.

Sometimes, the totality of the self and its inner dialogue of characters has been described as body, soul and spirit— or as body, mind and soul. Freud spoke of id, ego and superego. Secular rational intelligence is superficial and reductionist and tends to speak only of body and mind. Sometimes, as with Paul, the inner dialogue comprises a range as great or greater than Patrick White's. Paul speaks of body, mind, heart, psyche, soul, spirit,

168/Massacre of the innocent

will, flesh and so on. But whatever the description, all speak of human personhood as a continuity of some kind and an inner dialogue of some kind.

In the few lines I have cited from John's Gospel, we can see that he recognises that there is both continuity and inner dialogue in the personhood of God, too. He speaks of the *logos* which is with God and which is God. In time this insight, also shared by other first-century biblical writers as they reflected on the relationship between Jesus and God, would be put into a form of words known as the doctrine of the Trinity. These words would say that there is but one God (continuity), who is Creator (in family language 'Father'), Redeemer (in family language 'Son') and Sanctifier (or Holy Spirit).

These writers would also say that the Creator, the Redeemer and the Sanctifier are each fully God, but that God is, nevertheless, one not three. That is to say, on the higher plane of God's personhood, there is continuity and inner dialogue, but it is too complex and mysterious to put into words, except for words which produce seeming paradox and rational contradiction.

Given our inability, despite modern psychology, to understand the complexity of human personhood, it should come as no surprise that divine personhood is infinitely more complex and ultimately a permanent mystery. But both John and the more sophisticated Trinitarian theology that followed hold that it is God, all of God, who loves the world and acted in Jesus Christ to bring about reconciliation. There is no opposing of an angry 'Creator-Father' with a nice 'Redeemer-Son'.

Paul, too, is a first-century biblical author who views Christ's life and death in cosmic, eternal, mystical terms as one great act, purpose and intention of God. Like John, Paul discerns God's intentions revealed by Jesus Christ as pre-existent in God before the creation of the world (what we call the space–time universe). Also, like John, Paul says love is God's motivating energy; love for the creation and love for the human race in which the creation becomes conscious of itself.

In his letter to the followers of Christ's religion in ancient Ephesus, Paul praises God's eternal purpose:

> Blessed be the God and Father of our Lord Jesus Christ, who has blessed us in Christ with every spiritual blessing in the heavenly places, just as he chose us in Christ before the foundation of the world to be holy and blameless before him in love. He destined us for adoption as his children through Jesus Christ, according to the good pleasure of his will, to the praise of his glorious grace that he freely bestowed on us in the Beloved.
>
> In him, we have redemption through his blood, the forgiveness of our trespasses, according to the riches of his grace that he lavished on us. With all wisdom and insight he has made known to us the mystery of his will, according to his good pleasure that he set forth in Christ, as a plan for the fullness of time, to gather up all things in him, things in heaven and things on earth (chapter 1, verses 3 to 10).

Paul understands human redemption (from guilt, from alienation, from meaninglessness) as the eternal, divine intention of love revealed by the death of Christ ('his blood'). It is freely available, a 'lavished grace'. For Paul, the divine purpose will eventually reconcile all disharmonies on earth and in heaven. (This understanding of ultimate salvation is not unlike the visions of unity and harmony William James and Aldous Huxley 'saw' while under the influence of hallucinogens.)

For Paul and the other first-century interpreters of Christ, the death of Christ routs the powers of evil and disharmony through love. Christ does not oppose evil power with evil power, but with the power of self-sacrificial love. Perhaps in the modern era, no-one understood this better than India's Mahatma Gandhi. South Africa's Nelson Mandela came to understand it, too, perhaps during his long imprisonment. It cost Christ his life through a hideous, demeaning and excruciatingly painful form of execution.

For the original, first-century interpreters of Christ's death, Christ became a sacrifice of divine love on the altar of human sin and evil. Love is God's judgment on our sin. Christ taught that we should love our enemies and he himself practised what he preached to the very end— praying for the soldiers who crucified him: 'Father forgive them for they know not what they do' (Luke 23: 34).

Paul and his first-century colleagues do not see this sacrificial love as the love just of the man Jesus, but of the God-man Jesus. Because 'God was in Christ reconciling the world to himself', the suffering love of Jesus is also the suffering love of God. It is God, all of God, who reveals the mysterious, eternal purpose and reconciles all things through Christ. It is God's love for the world that quenches God's wrath against our sins. Salvation from sin and meaninglessness begins before creation because God's eternal purpose was always to reconcile with love all things in heaven and earth. Creation, time, space, history, society, incarnation, suffering, death, resurrection–ascension, eternal life are all part of one whole.

Irenaeus also views God's purposes as eternal. He interprets God's purpose for human beings as our transformation from spiritually and morally immature children to adult ripeness. To adapt some words of the German poet Reiner Maria Rilke, Irenaeus expects us as persons 'to grow and to grow until we die ripe into God'. But when is someone ripe? Jesus died at the relatively *young* age of thirty-three. Was he ripe? Age does not guarantee ripeness.

As a priest, over several decades I have visited the elderly in their homes, nursing homes, hospitals and retirement villages. My experience is that the elderly fall into two distinct categories— categories which are not so clearly visible at earlier stages of life. On the one hand, some of the elderly are the most open, kindly, generous and compassionate of all human beings I ever meet. But on the other hand, I encounter among the elderly a group that are the most selfish, bitter, twisted, closed and ungenerous of all human beings I know.

I suppose the origin of the clearer distinction is ageing itself. As we grow old what we are, the choices we have made, the reality we faced or the reality we failed to face become more obvious and harder to hide. I have seen children die 'ripe' and the elderly die green and hard. This would not surprise Irenaeus. But it is a fundamental error of secular, rational intelligence to equate fullness of life with longevity.

In the Sermon on the Mount, as written in Matthew's Gospel, Jesus says: 'Be perfect . . . as your heavenly Father is perfect.' According to Matthew, this saying comes at the conclusion of Christ's teaching that we must love our enemies. The word 'perfect' translated in most English versions of Matthew's Gospel actually means 'whole' or 'complete'. A better rendition, there- fore, is: 'Be whole and complete . . . as your heavenly Father is whole and complete.'

Becoming whole and complete is exactly how Irenaeus views God's eternal purpose for us. He sees love— the divine love, our love for others, including our love for enemies— as the path to wholeness and completeness. Love, not age, is what ripeness is about.

Carl Jung remained stuck with his distortion of the meaning of Christ's death. He could see that in some way the incarnation and the suffering of God in Jesus Christ was an answer to Job's challenge. But he could not grasp that answer fully because he was stuck with an angry God/nice Jesus. Hence, Jung saw God as divided against God— not good and loving, but a mixture of good and evil.

✠ God as a suffering God

Christ the suffering God-man is an answer to Job. Not a full and final answer. Still left unexplained is the necessity for the large amount of unjust suffering in the world or how the victims will be healed and made whole and complete.

The answer to Job is the image of God as a suffering God. It is not the image of a despot demanding submission, but the image of God as weeping, in pain, suffering with and for creation. This is the image Bonhoeffer had in mind when, thinking about the scientific and technological power of 'man come of age', he said, 'Only a suffering God will do'.

According to Matthew's parable of 'the Judgment of the Nations', Jesus taught that God is so identified with human suffering that human suffering is always God's suffering too. The Son of Man and the king in the parable represent Christ himself. All peoples and nations are judged by whether or not they have loved sufferers as Christ loves. To those who have so loved, the king says:

Come, you that are blessed by my Father, inherit the kingdom prepared for you from the foundation of the world; for
I was hungry and you gave me food, I was thirsty and you
gave me something to drink, I was a stranger and you
welcomed me, I was naked and you gave me clothing, I was
sick and you took care of me, I was in prison and you visited
me (chapter 25, verses 34 to 36).

To those who have not loved sufferers with the love of
Christ, the king in the parable says:

You that are accursed, depart from me into the eternal fire
prepared for the devil and his angels; for I was hungry and
you gave me no food, I was thirsty and you gave me nothing
to drink, I was a stranger and you did not welcome me,
naked and you did not give me clothing, sick and in prison
and you did not visit me (verses 41 to 43).

The parable says that when we fail to share our food with
the hungry, our drink with the thirsty, our clothing with the
naked, when we fail to visit the sick and those in prison, then
we fail to love God. We brutalise God and humanity.

In some profound sense, beyond reason and imagination's
comprehension, God is incarnate not just in the suffering and
death of Jesus Christ, but in all suffering and death. God is raped
when a woman is raped. God is battered when a child is battered.
God is thrashed for supposed masturbation when Arthur is
thrashed. This is the image of God that emerges from the
experience of the life, teachings, sufferings, death and resurrection–ascension of Jesus Christ.

It is a long time ago and I cannot remember exactly what I
did actually say to Gerry the journalist that Sunday morning

when he came to church wondering about the meaning of the cross. What I should have said was:

> Yes, Gerry, the cross does say something about God and suffering. You were right to become an atheist about your God of sunshine and flowers. In this world, there is lots of sunshine and there are lots of beautiful flowers, but there is cruelty, pain and accidents like the one that killed your sister, too. In the end, only a suffering God will do.
>
> We could never accept that God is good and loving when our sisters die at sixteen— unless, somehow, we could see God as part of their suffering and ours, too. The suffering God of love lavishes us with grace for our sins and participates in all the pain of our sufferings.

This is the reason why I said at the beginning of the last chapter: 'If it wasn't for Jesus Christ, I would believe in God, but I wouldn't trust God.'

But what about the damned? How does an intuitive, mystical, transcendent signal that damnation must be real square with the love of God? Any answer must be pure speculation. In my imagination, I see the damned in similar, but almost infinitely more complex, circumstances to those of us all. For God's love to take effect in our lives, we must repent of our sin, confess it and then claim God's lavish grace upon us. To repent and confess, we must relive our sins before God as a precursor to our total liberation from them.

I see the damned in the presence of Infinite Love having to experience everything their victims experienced as a precursor to their reconciliation with that Love. But they must intentionally will to do so. Willing it is up to them. The love is always there.

8.

Only love redeems

The meaning of life is not '42'

'THE MEANING OF LIFE IS TO JOURNEY FROM NAIVETY to innocence.' These are the words that popped out of my mouth at the pub after the Mount Vic Fliks. In the rest of this book, I will try to unravel what I take them to mean.

Patrick White concludes his self-portrait, *Flaws in the Glass*, with a small section entitled 'What is left?' This was written some thirty years after his slip-in-the-mud theophany and when he was almost seventy years of age. In part, he says:

> You reach a point where you have had everything and everything amounts to nothing. Only love redeems. I don't mean love in the Christian sense. To lavish what is seen as Christian love, indiscriminately on all mankind, is in the end as ineffectual as violence and hatred. Love in homeopathic doses can be more effective than indiscriminate slugs of the other doled out to a sick society. Christian love has lost its virtue, as antibiotics lose theirs through over-dosage.
>
> Christians will say I don't understand Christian love.
>
> Perhaps I don't; it is too grand a theory. When I say love redeems, I mean the love shared with an individual, not necessarily sexual, seductive though sexuality may be. Those

who believe I don't understand Christian love will probably
be joined by the ones who interpret this other statement as
the straw grabbed at by an ageing man as passion floats out
of reach. If it is making do, let us make do, in a world falling
apart.[1]

With these last brushstrokes of his self-portrait, White paints
himself with typical ambiguity— world-weary, satisfied but dissatisfied, despairing but not despairing, defiant but humble. I don't
think he does understand Christian love, but I have no desire to
be joined in criticising him by those who interpret his statement
'only love redeems' as geriatric straw-grabbing.

To the end of his life, Patrick White was a jumble of
contradictions about the Christian faith. In 1961, you will
recall, he ceased attending church because he 'found that
churches destroy the mystery of God'. In 1985, five years
before his death, he continued to maintain his long-standing
refusal to receive Holy Communion, even when seriously ill. On
this occasion, writing with explanation to a clergyman he obviously liked, he said:

> I am ashamed not to have answered your message before,
> but I have had a lot more illness since returning from hospital.
> Thank you for offering to bring us communion to the house.
> If I refuse the offer, it is because I cannot see myself as a
> true Christian. My faith is put together out of bits and pieces.
> I am a believer, but not the kind most 'Christians' would
> accept.[2]

In 1988, Sister Angela Solling, an engaging, complex, radical
Anglican nun from the Franciscan community of St Clare, visited
Patrick White and presented him with a 'holding cross'. This

cross, says David Marr, the editor of Patrick White's collected letters, 'he wore round his neck for the rest of his life'.[3]

Manoly Lascaris, Patrick White's life-long partner, is Greek Orthodox. Through Lascaris, White came into direct contact with Eastern Orthodox Christianity. I can understand White rejecting a church that had reached the dizzy depths of sermons banning 'Guess the number of beans in the jar' competitions. I can even understand him rejecting, as 'destroying the mystery of God', a church which turns Christ's religion into faith-castle belief in dogmas and obedience to moral rules. (Though it must be said that seers of no lesser vision than White's—for example, T.S. Eliot as an Anglican and Australia's Les Murray as a Catholic—have looked beyond the trivia and banality of their parish churches to the treasure trove of riches retained in their liturgies, scripture readings and sacraments.)

But it is not at all credible to me that White should include Eastern Christianity among the churches that 'destroy the mystery of God'.

✠ The Eastern church and the path of redemption

In Christian theology, there are two ways of talking about God—the positive way and the negative way. On the whole, the Western church has followed the former and the Eastern church the latter.

Thomas Aquinas' dictum that 'Whatever you can imagine God to be, that God is not' is a *bon mot* of the Western church, but is much neglected. Although the positive way is aware that God can be contained by no human thought, word or image, the positive way speaks of God, positively, by analogy. Thus, God is spoken of as Father, as Almighty, as the Creator. But these are all human analogies. At its crudest, especially with North American-type fundamentalism, the positive way images God as little more than a Superman. Even at its best, the positive way has become an obstacle to spiritual perception for the secularised, rational-intelligence mentality of the West.

For example, the positive analogy of God as 'Father' is so deeply embedded in the Western way of thinking that modern, feminist attempts to redress the inherent sexism of this analogy, by naming God also as 'Mother', have been met with outrage and murmurings of heresy. Aquinas' dictum is forgotten. Hence, it is lost to sight that 'Father' is simply an analogy of the positive way and that, in essence, God is not Father or Mother, but both/more than/neither.

Churchgoers in the West are either not aware or have forgotten (I think mostly the former) that their positive talk about God is analogical. Hence to secular, rational consciousness this talk sounds like fairytales or Freudian projection. Of course, there is nothing inherently wrong with speaking positively about God by analogy. But to avoid excessive literalism and misleading fundamentalism, the West needs a good dose of the negative way.

Eastern Christianity, with its emphasis on the negative way, stresses the absolute unknowability of God. Eastern Christianity does not say that God cannot be known at all. Both East and West accept that God is known by God's self-revelation, especially by God's self-revelation through the teaching and life of Jesus Christ.

However, whereas the West tends to use major doctrines, such as the incarnation or the Trinity, as teaching vehicles, implying 'this is what God is like', the East treats them as great mysteries to be contemplated. In the West, the tendency is to present these dogmas as beliefs necessary to salvation (the faith-castle leap). In the East, these dogmas are viewed as mystical antinomies, the end of our mind's reach, where rationality stops and contemplation and worship begin. Hence, in the West teaching is expected to be the channel which transmits the religion of Christ from one generation to the next. In the East, liturgy and participation in mystical worship is the expected transmission channel.

Unconsciously at least, a seer of Patrick White's intensity knew all this. With the walls of the entranceway to his house covered with Eastern icons, I cannot accept that he did not know it consciously, too. White's withdrawal back into the spiritual closet after his initial coming out seems to hide some deeper ambiguity about his wrestle with Christ's religion.

This ambiguity, and White's awareness of the essential mystery of God which is so cherished by Eastern Christianity, is voiced in what he writes about one of Lascaris' Greek aunts. Reading what follows, you may like to ask whether White is preaching to himself. If so, then, except perhaps for the glimmer of spiritual conviction expressed in the final sentence, the sermon did not take:

> Aunt Polymnia, Professor of Greek at the Sorbonne, who gave her life to education, was refused a pension for not having taken French nationality, went mad in consequence, and had to be brought back to Athens, where she spent her last days in the Asylum of the Sacred Girdle.
>
> Like most 'enlightened' Greeks, Polymnia was not a believer— superficially, that is. Even the most sceptical cling to the aesthetics, the history of Orthodoxy, until in a crisis,

whether some personal quarrel or national disaster, the blood and tears of faith come pouring out through supposedly healed wounds and open eyes.

The Greeks have survived through their Orthodox faith, professed or submerged. It is also why an unlikely relationship between an Orthodox Greek and a lapsed Anglican egotist agnostic pantheist occultist existentialist would-be, though failed Christian Australian has lasted forty years.[4]

Aunt Polymnia epitomises White's 'professed unbelievers' who are afraid that, by openly admitting their own unprofessed faith, they 'will forfeit their right to be considered intellectuals'. In inverted commas, she is 'enlightened'. Polymnia possesses 'supposedly', but not actually, healed wounds and open eyes. 'Superficially' she is not a believer, White says.

Clearly, Patrick White perceives in the Eastern Christianity of the Greeks something of an intuitive, mystical religion that is his soul's desire and his mind's truth. But he continues to say that he himself is, yet is not, a Christian— 'a would-be, though failed Christian'; 'a believer, but not the kind most "Christians" would accept.'

For Polymnia and the Greeks, he acknowledges the value of being part of a great spiritual tradition, but he himself withdraws into the spiritual closet. Why? The inconsistency is something one wants more to understand than to criticise.

✠ God's love is unconditional

Whilst writing this particular part of my book during sabbatical leave granted for the purpose, I have been called out to attend the funeral of one of my diocese's retired priests. He was a much-loved, gentle pastor.

Because I am on sabbatical leave, I do not take my usual part in leading the service. Instead, I sit with the congregation. I arrive ten minutes before the service is to begin and kneel in my place with my face in my hands.

I have had several weeks alone in the solitude of my writing room and I sense a Presence here in church which I have missed greatly. It is not a presence of place as such. I do not hold the superstition that God is more present in church buildings than in kitchens, living or writing rooms. But the Presence is invoked by the symbolism of the place: candles flickering on the altar and on the coffin; plummeting but soft music drifting from the organ; sunlight shining through stained-glass windows, reflecting aureole-like onto the heads and faces of the assembled congregation; a respectful hush and the occasional quiet whisper from those gathered. Even the sermon, because it is simple, direct and gently spoken, invokes the Presence.

For his text, the preacher chooses Psalm 31, verse 5:

Into your hand I commend my spirit;
you have redeemed me O Lord,
faithful God.

The preacher reminds us that these words were written more than three thousand years ago and that centuries later they would appear, in Luke's Gospel, on the lips of Christ as he expires on the cross. We all think of the loving priest and pastor we are saluting with the final farewell.

I returned to my writing more puzzled than ever about Patrick White, the 'would-be, though failed Christian'. Why, when apparently he could see what was needed, did he withdraw into spiritual privacy and play, ironically and ambiguously, at being a Christian, yet not being a Christian? Why could he say 'only love redeems' and then immediately reject the love of Christ? Is the problem the Christian faith or is it something in Patrick White himself?

Paul Tillich, the German-American theologian, says:

> You can't love another person until you love yourself and you can't love yourself until you accept that God loves you.

Secular psychologists would probably agree with the first part of what Tillich says. If we don't love ourselves, then our relationships with others are likely to be those either of dominance or of submission. Christ's Golden Rule, 'You shall love your neighbour as you love yourself', recognises this. If we lack self-love, we seek worth in others' eyes by being bullies or doormats. We cannot love another unless we are at peace with our own self.

Tillich says that we cannot have such peace until we accept God's love for us. Otherwise, he implies, we are forever at war within ourselves, contending with our ambition, self-hate, hunger for wealth, failure, disappointment, status seeking, power-mongering, fear of relationships— or whatever else we think will bring us to blessed satisfaction or cause us to lose it.

Part of Patrick White's ambivalence about Christianity is the apparent difficulty he had with accepting himself as worthy of God's love.

'Grace' is the usual word which the religion of Christ uses to speak about God's love. It defines a warts-and-all kind of love, a love that God gives lavishly and bounteously, regardless of merit in the beloved. The kind of love St Francis demonstrated when, heedless of his own health, he kissed the leper. The kind of love Mother Theresa showed to beggars dying unnoticed by the passing crowd on the streets of Calcutta. The kind of love Jesus expressed when he prayed for his executioners, 'Father, forgive them, for they know not what they do'. Grace is a love without conditions, an unconditional love.

This is the love Patrick White, I think, had difficulty accepting: not because it was 'too grand a theory', as he claims, but because of a perversity in his own character.

Early in his self-portrait, White says:

> Alas, my inability to forgive is a trait I must have inherited from my Uncle James.[5]

There is no elaboration. It is characteristic of White's self-honesty that he even mentions it at all. Yet for a person so intensely given to self-knowledge, one might expect more than a glib genetic explanation. Is there not even the shadow of a possibility that he was possessed of an unwillingness, not just an inability, to forgive? And as we do not inherit genetic traits from uncles, is White being ironically evasive or self-delusory?

Shortly after the publication of *Flaws in the Glass*, White elaborated on his 'inability' in a letter to Geoffrey Dutton, one of his most long-standing friends. (Ironically, within months White 'cut' Dutton for good, bolting the door of forgiveness and reconciliation solidly shut.) He comments to Dutton:

> I did say early on in the book that my inability to forgive is probably inherited from my Uncle James, who never came near us again after my mother received him in a sleeveless dress, when they returned to Australia after my birth. This inability

to forgive is one of my worst flaws and, every time I come
to the bit about forgiveness in the Lord's Prayer, I know I
can't pretend to be a Christian—as I admit in the book.[6]

The 'bit about forgiveness' in Christ's prayer to which White
refers is, of course, 'forgive us our sins as we forgive those who
sin against us'.

Whether its source was an 'inability' or an unwillingness,
Patrick White certainly nurtured a profound difficulty about
forgiving others. His life was studded with broken friendships.
For some fault, flaw or perceived slight which he supposed was
their sin alone, he would reject, permanently, family members
and close friends. They were 'cut'—regardless, for example in
Dutton's case, of the length of the relationship or of the overtures
which they made to White seeking reconciliation. Often, as in
the case of the painter Sidney Nolan, who was 'cut' after the
suicide of his first wife Cynthia, it is hard not to see the fault as
solely White's own.

White confessed to Dutton that his inability to forgive was
one of his 'worst flaws'. Naming it a flaw, not a sin, perpetuates
his theory of genetic inheritance and absolves him of personal
responsibility for it. But this explanation smells fishy. If he wasn't
responsible for it, then, of course, there is no sin! One doesn't
ask God's forgiveness for having blue eyes or a bald head! But he
tells Dutton that he baulks at praying 'forgive us our sins as we
forgive those who sin against us' and says that this is why he
can't pretend to be a Christian.

This has more the feel of unwillingness, not 'inability', about
it. Was it the case that Patrick White wanted to be a Christian,
but was unwilling to fulfil the condition of being a forgiver? This

would explain his forty-plus years of ambivalence and ambiguity about the Christian faith.

At the end of the self-portrait, we hear White say 'only love redeems', and he then goes on immediately to reject Christian love as 'too grand a theory'. There was, though, this qualification:

> Christians will say I don't understand Christian love. Perhaps I don't . . .[1]

Paul Tillich says that to receive divine love is 'to accept that we are accepted in spite of our sins'. This is a classic understanding of God's grace. Did White, the 'would-be, though failed Christian', understand this? Did he think, instead, that divine forgiveness was conditional upon his ability or willingness to forgive others? Did he understand grace as unconditional love? Did he perceive that it is the forgiven who (slowly) learn to forgive, that it is the loved who love?

Did White understand the proper sequence of grace? Spiritually self-exiled from a great tradition, spiritually tucked away in a private closet— did he lack this vision?

St John, the mystical New Testament writer, explains the proper sequence of grace this way:

> Beloved, let us love one another, because love is from God; everyone who loves is born of God and knows God. Whoever does not love does not know God, for God is love. God's love was revealed among us this way: God sent his only Son into the world, so that we might live through him.
>
> In this is love, not that we loved God, but that he loved us and sent his Son to be the atoning sacrifice for our sins. Beloved, since God loved us so much, we also

ought to love one another. No one has ever seen God; if we love one another, God lives in us and his love is perfected in us.[7]

It seems to me that Patrick White did not understand Christian love in this way. He appears to think that he had to *perfect* his own love in order to be worthy of divine grace. If this were the case, then the whole human race would be precluded from receiving divine grace by their 'inability' to forgive others.

Of course, it is possible that White did actually understand the proper sequence of grace— that he knew by accepting God's love he would change and become more forgiving, and that he didn't want this. Who can know, except God and Patrick White's own soul? But my guess is that he did not understand.

✠ God's love is at the heart of the meaning of life

White's recognition that 'only love redeems' is the very essence of life's meaning according to the religion of Christ. To Western secular ears, the question, 'What is the meaning of life?', appears too big and complex to tackle. Scepticism about the faintest possibility of an answer is so great that cynical, humorous send-up has become the only credible response. Hence the joke that the meaning of life is 42.

It does not seem to have occurred to the world of secular rational intelligence that the problem may lie not with the question, but with the kind of answer which is expected. When secular rational intelligence asks, 'What is the meaning of life?', it expects an answer in the form of a theorem or explanation. With such an expectation, '42' is a fine answer, because it cynically exposes the impossibility of human omniscience. For how could we know the meaning of life in this way unless we understood all things from the beginning to the end? For those expecting a theorem–explanation answer, '57' or '1319' would be as effective as '42' in reminding them that God alone is the Alpha and the Omega, the first and the last, the beginning and the end.

Even in everyday life, it is not theorems and explanations which give meaning to our lives, but experiences of personal worth, value and significance. Presumably, this is what Patrick White means by saying that love shared with an individual redeems and that 'only love redeems'. He recognises that critics will reject this statement as mere straw-grabbing by a passion-diminished geriatric. Presumably, these anticipated critics are secular intellectuals who view White's redeeming love as a mere candle flame held against the winds of meaninglessness, which blast from their now relinquished and futile searches for redemption by theorems and explanations.

To know the meaning of life as an explanation would be to know everything. That prerogative is God's alone, though there are some physicists who, in their hubris, still expect to formulate a final theory which will explain everything— 'everything' excluding, presumably, their own ordinary rational consciousness, which does the formulating, as well as those other forms of consciousness which they choose to ignore!

Aldous Huxley and William James, you will recall, believed that their drug-induced altered states of consciousness exposed them to previously undreamt of experiences of reality and purpose. James was filled both with wonder and apprehension: wonder at the depths of being not perceived by ordinary rational consciousness and apprehension about the absence of a map for these vast new territories.

Huxley at first equated his experience with ultimate salvation. Later, he modified this view to say that what he experienced was simply sufficient to demonstrate beyond doubt that there is a purpose to human life, which will eventuate in total fulfilment. James 'saw' the reconciliation of all contraries and disharmonies— a unity of all things— and was also convinced that we live in a meaningful universe. Both Huxley and James thus came to view religion in a new light.

Negative or mystical theology emphasises that we can never know God in the sense of comprehending God intellectually but, paradoxically, what we can know of God by the practice of the negative way is so overwhelmingly purposive and positive that no human language can capture and express it.

This way of thinking is totally foreign to the Western mind. We have been so thoroughly schooled to accept (or reject) the positive way of speaking about God that to define God's character negatively seems incomprehensible, even nonsense.

When we started the Eremos Institute, we invited people to come away for weekend guided retreats. A friend lent us a house for this purpose on the headland of MacMasters Beach, about one-and-a-half hours' drive north of Sydney. It is a beautiful unspoilt coastal area— a large national park, with many walking trails and secluded beaches nearby. About once a month, people came with us for a guided retreat, people from all walks of life— students, teachers, office workers, doctors, carpenters, lawyers— a cross-section of Australian society.

Saturday afternoons were always given over to total silence. Most participants had difficulty with understanding and accepting this at first. Often the level of fearful apprehension was palpable. In everyday life, the world of these retreatants was filled with activity, conversation and sound. We were inviting them to participate in the opposite: in passivity, receptiveness, solitude and silence. No talk, no radio, no CD player, no television— not even a book. Just to be alone and to be silent.

We understood the fearful apprehension. When it is not necessary, most of our everday activity, talk and sound is distraction. Solitude and silence condemn us to ourselves. Fear derives from anticipating the experience as loneliness and self-confrontation. But as the mystical way understands, solitude and silence open the self to God's presence, to the Other. It is a way of knowing.

Eremos invented some simple slogans to assist those for whom the notion of solitude and silence was a fearful mystery. We would say: 'You can never know God more deeply than you know yourself. If you don't know yourself, then you can't know God.' We always suggested that, during the silence, a couple of hours be spent in the one place— sitting on the beach, under a gum tree, on a cliff top or wherever. We advised that, during this time, retreat participants should not attempt to think, meditate or pray, but to relax and 'be', to 'let what comes up come up'.

This latter slogan, 'to let what comes up come up', evolved from many failed attempts to explain how to allow one's stream of consciousness to flow unimpeded.

Those participating usually wanted to know what they should do, or what they should think about or meditate on, during the silence. They found it difficult to accept the recommendation to do nothing except 'be', to 'let what comes up come up'. A slogan which was helpful to some, but not others, was: 'Waste time with God.' But, after emphasising the need to relax, to let go, to stop trying, the slogan 'let come up what comes up' proved the most effective for conveying the essence of the silence and solitude experience.

On Saturday evenings, after a celebratory dinner-party, those who so wished were given opportunity to speak about their experience during the silence and solitude. Invariably, people had 'peak' experiences not dissimilar to Huxley's and James' drug-induced experiences. But there was a crucial difference. These mystical experiences were continuous with everyday life and the person's usual sense of self. In the language used earlier in this book, these experiences proved to be inner-worldly, not other-worldly, experiences. It seems to be characteristic of the artificial, drug-induced states that they are *dis*continuous with everyday life and lead to loss of the ordinary self.

Guided retreats are just one way by which mystical experiences introduce people to depths of reality and meaning unavailable to ordinary, everyday, rational consciousness. These experiences evoke understanding, personal worth and significance; they do not provide theorems or explanations. They are naturally available altered states of consciousness that neither damage physical health nor create discontinuity with ordinary life. A saying of the Eastern church, 'We retreat in order to return', captures the wholeness of this inner-worldly mysticism. But love, not 'peak' experiences or self-knowledge, is the heart of Christ's religion. Christianity is the mysticism of love.

When Patrick White says 'only love redeems', he is saying exactly what the religion of Christ says. The only difference is that White limits himself to an individual, human love, whereas Christ speaks of a divine, all-pervading love.

✠ Love's liberation

Seen from the perspective of his humanity, the story of Jesus is the story of a man totally abandoning himself to love. He does not give explanations; he loves. He preaches a kingdom of God, by which he means that there is a divine purpose which runs from eternity, through space and time, to eternity. The governance of this kingdom is the governance of love.

Jesus himself embodies this kingdom by his own all-encompassing love. A love which embraces the stigmatised and the afflicted. A love which embraces lepers, women, underclass workers, traitors, adulterers and soldiers. A love which demands enemies become friends. A love which eschews sentimentality and condemns the hypocrite, the abuser and the exploiter.

As the Gospels tell the story, Jesus knew he would be undone by the lack of human love. In his sufferings on the cross, he even wondered if he had been mistaken about love and cried out, 'My God, my God, why have you forsaken me?' His resurrection appearances from eternity back into space and time were interpreted by his first disciples as confirmation of the divine kingdom.

The first-century followers of Christ experienced God's love so deeply that, despite the ignominy of their Master's death, the danger to their own lives from the 'powers' that had Jesus killed, their forebodings of personal sin and guilt, they felt liberated to face anything or anyone, including God. Thus John wrote:

> God is love, and those who abide in love abide in God, and God abides in them. Love has been perfected among us in this: that we may have boldness on the day of judgment because as he [Jesus] is, so are we in this world. There is no fear in love, but perfect love casts out fear.[8]

Carl Jung's scatological challenge to God liberated him for life from all fear because, through it, he learnt to abandon himself totally to God's grace. Abandonment to grace is what Paul meant when he said salvation is by grace through faith. Faith, for him, was not blind faith-leap belief, but self-abandonment to God as love. He, too, experienced liberation from all fear and wrote about it movingly:

> If God is for us, who is against us? He who did not withhold his own Son, but gave him up for all of us, will he not with him also give us everything else? . . . Who will separate us from the love of Christ? Will hardship, or famine, or nakedness, or peril, or sword? . . . No, in all these things we are more than conquerors through him who loved us. For I am convinced that neither death, nor life, nor angels, nor rulers, nor things present, nor things to come, nor powers, nor height, nor depth, nor anything else in all creation, will be able to separate us from the love of God in Christ Jesus our Lord.[9]

✠ Only love redeems

I suspect that in the depth of our being, we all do know that 'only love redeems', that love alone makes life worthwhile and gives it purpose and meaning. Without love, all our scientific, artistic and spiritual achievements are as straw. Time, tide and entropy will carry them all away.

But secular consciousness has no language, no story, no poem, no map by which to interpret our smaller loves onto a larger canvas of love. By expecting explanations, it misses the point and dismisses White's statement, 'only love redeems', as geriatric whistling against the wind.

I have argued that Patrick White did not understand Christian love at its central point, at the point of abandonment to grace. But is there another reason, too, for his vehement rejection of Christian love towards the end of his life? Why, for example, could he not accept his experience of redemption through the love of an individual as a theophany, as anticipatory of a greater redeeming Love? Why was it, for him, *either* individual love *or* Christian love? Why was it either/or, not both/and?

There is, I think, another reason. It is to be found in that classic writing on Christian mystical love, *The Cloud of Unknowing.*

9.

Cloud of unknowing

Waiting in the darkness for light

T HE BOOK, *THE CLOUD OF UNKNOWING*, IS AN ANONYMOUS, fourteenth-century piece of mystical writing, published at a time when Western Christianity was locked into the dry rationalism known as Scholasticism. Although the unknown author is English, *The Cloud* expresses the theology of Eastern, not Western, Christianity. It draws especially on the writings of Pseudo-Dionysus, an anonymous sixth-century Syrian monk who wrote under the pseudonym 'Dionysus'.

Where Scholasticism was rigorously rationalistic, *The Cloud* adopts the negative way to explain Christ's religion. It totally rejects reason as a path to God. With Patrick White's jaundiced opinion of intellectuals and their rationalistic way of viewing religion, and with his own high evaluation of intuitive knowing, it is not surprising that White called *The Cloud* 'a very seductive little book'.[1]

The Cloud does not teach that we are able to know God by our own efforts; on the contrary, it says that God initiates our knowing God. But it is a knowing not of reason, but of love. White would make good sense of this. His own slip-in-the-mud theophany was an unexpected gift of grace. All theophanies, by definition, are gifts of grace— they are manifestations of God by God. What *The Cloud* does teach is that we know God by the desire of love, not by the desire of reason.

In order to pursue the desire of love, reason must be abandoned. Reason, says *The Cloud*, is useful for understanding the ordinary world, but useless for knowing and understanding God. Writing as a mentor to a novice, the author says:

> For whoever hears or reads about all this, and thinks it fundamentally an activity of the mind, and proceeds then to work it all out along these lines, is on quite the wrong track. He manufactures an experience that is neither spiritual, nor physical. He is dangerously misled and in real peril. So much so that, unless God in his great goodness intervenes with a miracle of mercy and makes him stop and submit to the advice of those who really know, he will go mad or suffer some other dreadful form of spiritual mischief and devilish deceit. Indeed, almost casually as it were, he may be lost eternally, body and soul. So for the love of God be careful, and do not attempt to achieve this experience intellectually.[2]

To abandon reason and nurture the desire of love, says the author, one must enter the cloud of [reason's] unknowing:

> Lift up your heart to God with humble love: and mean God himself, and not what you get out of him . . .
>
> When you first begin, you find only darkness, and as it were a cloud of unknowing . . .
>
> Reconcile yourself to wait in this darkness as long as is necessary, but still go on longing after him you love . . .[3]

✠ Simone Weil and *The Cloud*'s inner-worldly mysticism

In the twentieth century, Simone Weil is a person who intuitively came to the same conclusions as *The Cloud*. Weil was a contemporary of Jean Paul Sartre and Simone de Beauvoir. With them, she ranks not only as one of the finest minds of twentieth-century France, but of Europe also. Each had the same rigorous training in philosophy and each branched out into other intellectual fields.

Sartre and de Beauvoir remained all their lives in their intellectuality and atheism, creating a cult following around the world. Weil is still known only in fairly restricted academic and spiritual circles, but one suspects that hers will be the more lasting contribution to human life and values.

Like Aunt Polymnia, initially Weil was one of Patrick White's 'enlightened' intellectuals. Given to endless hours of reading and study, all her life she suffered from intense, debilitating headaches. When it came to the question of God, Weil's rationalistic intellectuality could see nothing except an insoluble problem—the interminable 'Does God exist?' debate.

She was attracted to the English metaphysical poet George Herbert, especially to his poem 'Love bade me welcome, but my soul drew back'. The intellectual insolubility of the problem of God became, in due course, her own personal cloud of unknowing. It was from the darkness of that cloud she came to 'know' God for the first time. Of this experience she says:

> At a moment of intense physical pain while I was making the effort to love, although believing I had no right to give any name to the love, I felt while completely unprepared for it (I had never read the mystics), a presence more personal, more certain, and more real than that of a human being; it

was inaccessible both to sense and imagination, and it resembled the love that irradiates the tenderest smile of somebody one loves . . .

In my arguments about the insolubility of the problem of God, I had never foreseen the possibility of that, of a real contact, person to person, here below, between a human being and God. I had vaguely heard tell of things of this kind, but I had never believed in them.[4]

Simone Weil devoted her life to love. She obtained employment as a factory worker in order to identify with labourers suffering the affliction of tedious, exhausting, poorly-paid, physical work. She died prematurely in 1943, aged thirty-four, having damaged her health irreparably by refusing to eat properly whilst people in German-occupied France were dying of hunger. She is, and is more and more being recognised as, a great mystic of God's love.

Six centuries before Weil's vision of love, the author of *The Cloud* was stressing that God is known by love, not intellect. In very strong words, he says:

All rational beings, angels and men, possess two faculties, the power of knowing and the power of loving. To the first, to the intellect, God who made them is forever unknowable, but to the second, to love, he is completely knowable, and that by every separate individual. So much so that one loving soul by itself, through its love, may know for itself him who is incomparably more than sufficient to fill all souls that exist.[5]

✠ Patrick White and *The Cloud*'s other-worldly mysticism

Patrick White came across *The Cloud of Unknowing* in 1970, nearly twenty years after his slip-in-the-mud theophany and ten years before he wrote his self-portrait *Flaws in the Glass*.

He refers to *The Cloud* in the same letter in which he said that he hoped his books would 'give professed unbelievers glimpses of their own unprofessed faith'. He was attracted by the book, but found problems for himself with its teachings. He says:

> The other day, I picked up a copy of a very seductive little book called *The Cloud of Unknowing*. It is written by a 14th century English mystic, and deals with the contemplative life. I can't go all the way with it, because I feel that the moral flaws in myself are more than anything my creative source.[6]

It is hard to fathom what White means by his 'moral flaws'. Is he thinking here, too, of his inability to forgive? Is he thinking of his homosexuality? Neither seems likely, because a few days later he wrote to Sidney Nolan, saying of *The Cloud*:

> A fascinating book, but what it proposes would be the end of us.[7]

Nolan was not known either for an inability to forgive or as a homosexual. What White and Nolan had in common was their creative art— as painter and as novelist. But what, in *The Cloud*'s teaching, would be 'the end' of them?

Certainty is impossible, but most likely White's difficulty is the eventual drift of *The Cloud*'s teaching into an other-worldly mysticism. As said earlier, the religion of Jesus Christ is an inner-worldly mysticism. But *The Cloud* negates not only reason, but the world, too. The love which it commends, as the only way to know God, is a disembodied, *other-worldly* love. As well as putting reason behind us by entering the cloud of unknowing, says the author, we must also put the world aside by entering the 'cloud of forgetting':

If ever you are to come to this cloud and live and work in it, as I suggest, then just as this cloud of unknowing is as it were above you, between you and God, so you must also put a cloud of forgetting between you and all creation.[8]

The author explains that the 'cloud of forgetting' applies not only to the material things of the world, but also to all that is sensuous— states of being and emotion. Thus, the marriage of heaven and earth, consummated by the incarnation of Christ, becomes a chaste divorce.

Patrick White must have found very attractive the idea of love, not reason, as the pathway to God. He valued intuition above reason and understood love's redeeming power— hence his comment that *The Cloud* is 'a very seductive little book'. But the world-negating mysticism of the 'cloud of forgetting' would indeed be the end of painters and novelists, whose art depends on sensuous imagery.

There is another piece of evidence which supports the view that *The Cloud*'s rejection of the world, as essential for experiencing the love of God, is White's problem with it. The letter in which he describes *The Cloud* as 'a very seductive little book' is also the letter in which he says:

The churches defeat their own aims, I feel, through the banality of their approach, and by rejecting so much that is sordid and shocking which can still be related to religious experience.[9]

Quite specifically and deliberately, *The Cloud* teaches rejection, not transformation, of all that is sordid and shocking. The whole world is placed in this category.

If this interpretation is correct, then the Christian love which White rejects as 'too grand a theory' is the bloodless spirituality of the 'cloud of forgetting'. If White thinks that this is the way to find the love of God, as taught by Christ, then it becomes impossible for him to view human love, including sexual love, as a theophany or sacrament of the greater divine love.

'Only love redeems' becomes the false choice of God or the world—an either/or. Incarnate love, which is both human and divine, is ruled out.

✠ The other-worldly character of much modern Christianity

Other-worldly mysticism is a continuing plague upon the house of Christ's religion. As part of my training for the Anglican ministry in the early 1960s, I was required to undertake what was called 'The Hospital Course'. Nowadays, it is a larger and more sophisticated element of clergy training called 'Clinical and Pastoral Education'. It meant spending three weeks in a hospital, becoming familiarised with its procedures, whilst visiting and spiritually ministering to patients.

My appointment was to Royal Prince Alfred Hospital, a large university teaching hospital adjacent to the University of Sydney. A member of the hospital staff was assigned to look after us, show us around and provide loose supervision. I was twenty-two at this time.

The person appointed as my supervisor was a female Jewish social worker of about thirty years of age, whose name I have now forgotten. The course itself was quite exciting and parts of it, such as witnessing in the operating theatre a caesarean birth, remain vivid in my memory. But more vivid, and critical for my personal life, is my memory of the Jewish social worker.

As well as its intellectual rigour, the Anglican Christianity of

my theological college possessed a strong streak of English puritanism in which I never felt comfortable. It was fearful of all
things sensual, including, and especially, the emotions, the arts
and sexuality. Its standard of biblical scholarship was high and 'in
the head'; its religion was not ascetic or other-worldly.

Thus, for example, I am indebted to its scholarship for being
able to read the New Testament through original Jewish and not
later Greek eyes. In Jewish eyes, 'the world' and 'the body' are
wholesome and good. They may be subject to sinful misuse, but
they are not in themselves corrupt or unspiritual. In later Greek
eyes, eyes which distorted the vision of Jesus the Jew, 'the world'
and 'the body' are evil and unspiritual in themselves. Intellectually, my college freed me from reading the New Testament
through the warped vision of Greek ascetic philosophy, which
came to dominate Christianity through theologians such as
Jerome and Augustine.

But what was taught at college was not practised. For
example, we were explicitly advised never to trust our emotions.
Emotions were viewed as scatty and sensual, reason alone as
trustworthy and reliable. Sexuality was taught as 'ethics in the
head', but its sensual ecstasy, or the complexities of actual human
relationships, were met with a repressive silence. We were
strongly advised to read only nice books and to see only nice
films, 'nice' meaning that which contained nothing sordid or
shocking.

Accepting this puritanism in my mind, but not in my heart,
led to some callous behaviour of my own in the real world of
the sordid and the shocking. Acting from my head, I dumped a
girlfriend with whom there was intense and tender mutual love,
because our relationship had become too sensual and sexual.

No matter what my heart felt—and it was unreliable anyway, wasn't it?—my head said that that kind of love could not redeem.

But I felt no guilt, had no foreboding of unredemption when, after seeking and gaining commitment from another girlfriend, I dumped her almost the next day. She was a very attractive person, much admired by other men. Clearly, obtaining her commitment was nothing but an ego trip of my own. I ought to have felt mortified and in deep shame about my destructive sin against her, but my (false) conscience was clear because our relationship was neither sensual nor sexual. I did not understand then, but later I came to see, that I was acting from Plato's, not Christ's, view of sin.

At Royal Prince Alfred Hospital, my Jewish supervisor was both sensual and spiritual. There was nothing in her of the English (or if I had been Catholic—Irish?) puritanism which fears sensuality as a threat to spirituality. I was not in love with her, but I was captivated by her living example of the marriage of heaven and earth, of the spiritual and the sensual. I am myself the son of a Jewish mother, so perhaps it is not merely superstitious to think my discomfort with puritanism was genetic as well as intuitive.

Experiencing this woman's life as a relaxed integration of flesh and spirit allowed me for the first time to actually feel the embodiment and inner-worldliness of Jesus the Jew's mysticism. Her integration expressed itself in her body language, dress, grooming, ease with herself as a sexual woman, ease in talking about God and religion, her verbal and physical demonstration of love for others, her celebration of life, including the whole gamut of emotions from joy to pain.

Nietzsche's words, which I had recently read but have now forgotten where, came to mind:

His [Jesus'] disciples will have to look more saved if I am to believe in their Saviour.

I recall thinking 'yes'.

The false image of Christ's religion as an other-worldly mysticism which is opposed to the sensual is a great obstacle to its acceptance in modern, secular society. Human, including sexual, love is prevented by this image from becoming a taste of the divine love itself. As a consequence, romantic love is called upon to fill our soul's deepest longings. It cannot bear this weight of expectation and hence romance fails and relationships fall apart.

The beauty of the world, the pain and sordidness of life, are not viewed as experiences to be transmuted spiritually into higher levels of personal integration, but as ends in themselves: sometimes briefly ecstatic ends and sometimes wallowingly hurtful ends. God is not worshipped in the midst of life, but retired to a far-off heaven or boxed up in a private closet. People such as Patrick White are made to feel that their human love is a mere grasping at straws of meaning, rather than a theophany of meaning and love in itself.

✠ Simone Weil's integration of inner-worldly mysticism

Simone Weil was ascetic in her personal self-denial of worldly pleasure but, paradoxically, thoroughly inner-worldly in her general practice and understanding of Christ's religion. She says:

> Never since the dawn of history, except for a certain period of the Roman Empire, has Christ been so absent as today. The separation of religion from the rest of social life, which seems natural even to the majority of Christians nowadays, would have been judged monstrous by antiquity.[10]

Weil viewed the sensate world as a veil which can both hide and reveal God. For her, the veil was most lifted in the extremes of our experience:

> Joy and suffering are two equally precious gifts which must both of them be fully tasted, each one in its purity and without trying to mix them. Through joy, the beauty of the world penetrates our soul. Through suffering, it penetrates our body. We could no more become friends of God through joy alone than one becomes a ship's captain by studying books on navigation.
>
> The body plays a part in all apprenticeships. On the plane of physical sensibility, suffering alone gives us contact with that necessity which constitutes the order of the world, for pleasure does not involve an impression of necessity . . . In order that a new sense may be formed in us which allows us to hear the universe as the vibration of the word of God, the transforming power of suffering and joy is equally indispensable.
>
> When either of them comes to us, we have to open the very centre of our souls to it, as a woman opens her door to messengers from her beloved. What does it matter to a lover if the messenger is courteous or rough, so long as he gives her a message?[11]

Love is ineffable. Weil's mystical experience of God's love always remained the central fact of her life. She sought ways, as do lovers, of expressing the ineffable. At the human level, when we are deeply, madly in love, overwhelmed, how do we express what we feel?

All conventional endearments— 'darling', 'sweetheart'— seem hollow. Language itself appears limited, inadequate, confining. Even saying a thousand times 'I love you' touches but the surface of what is experienced.

Our love is too great for words; it silences speech. How much more impossible it is to shape words expressive of the divine love. A mistress of language and image, Weil sought many ways to express her mystical experience of God's love. For example, attempting to fuse heart and intellect, she says:

> The infinity of space and time separates us from God. How can we seek for him? How can we go towards him? Even if we were to walk for endless centuries, we should do no more than go round and round the world . . .
>
> Over the infinity of space and time, the infinitely more infinite love of God comes to possess us. He comes at his own time. We have the power to consent to receive him or to refuse. If we remain deaf, he comes back again and again a beggar, but also, like a beggar, one day he stops coming. If we consent, God places a little seed in us and he goes away again.
>
> From that moment God has no more to do; neither have we, except to wait. We have only not to regret the consent we gave, the nuptial Yes. It is not as easy as it seems, for the growth of the seed within us is painful . . .[12]

✠ Only infinite love can redeem infinitely

I entirely agree with Patrick White that 'only love redeems'. But only an infinite love can redeem infinitely. It is by experiencing God's love, not via theorems or explanations, that we discover the meaning of life. As to explanations, we will always remain in a cloud of unknowing.

Life is full of meaning when we are romantically in love—not because of theories or explanations, but because of the worth, value and significance which lovers reciprocate to each other's hearts and souls. Seeming to defy rationalistic logic, but not the logic of love, this sense of value and worth spills over into all of life; everything we are and everything we do is transfigured, is suffused with meaning.

But even if a human love lasts with intensity for a lifetime, which it seldom does, ageing and the anticipation of death reveal its limited redemption. Only the experience of God's love can bestow infinite worth, value and significance. Only God's love is free from death's menacing prophecy of separation. Only God's love lavishes all of life, including our sufferings, with meaning.

In my lifetime— I am now fifty-four— I have met face-to-face only one person whom I would call a saint. By 'saint' I mean a person in whose life the love of God almost literally shines. I have met many people who thought they were saints, but without exception they were pious prigs.

I met Isobel Reilly during my first church appointment as an ordained priest. This was a two-year appointment in a bland middle-class suburb of Sydney. I was twenty-three at the time and Isobel seemed old, but I guess she was only in her early forties. Among the lawn-trimmed, neatly gardened, red-brick bungalows typical of the area, Isobel's house stood out. Weeds grew where everyone else had lawn and garden. Her house was weatherboard, paint-peeling, tumbledown and totally unprepossessing. I have no clear memory of whether she rented or owned it except a vague and uncertain recollection about her inheriting it from her father.

Physically, Isobel was ugly. She was short in stature, her hair lank and grey, her back hugely humped, her skin motley and her face distorted by a pronounced hairlip and cleft palate. When I met her, she was in remission from cancer, her only income a government pension.

With all these handicaps to normal social acceptability and to a confident, personal self-identity, one would anticipate Isobel might be a reclusive nobody, depressed and despairing in the sea of middle-class respectability and affluence around her. When I first called on her, as part of my parish visitation program, I was expecting to provide a little comfort to a lonely, isolated individual.

I discovered that over many years Isobel had persuaded the Child Welfare Department of the state government to place in her care unwanted, unadoptable babies. (This was still in the days when pregnant unmarried girls mostly signed over their babies for adoption by 'respectable' families; babies which were unadoptable were those the 'respectable' families would not take, babies with some kind of serious physical problem— blind, deaf or crippled of limb.) My memory is that Isobel would have two, sometimes three, of these babies at a time— though usually it was just one.

Although she was Anglican and attended church when her small charges permitted, as soon as Isobel received a new baby, she would be immediately on the 'phone to every priest and minister in the district. Each would receive a call 'telling' him (it was only 'him' back then) that she had a new baby, its name, and that he and his congregation were to pray for the child. This was done most forcefully. Isobel's ecumenical spirit demonstrated a spiritual largesse far beyond the sectarian suspicions of the churches in that suburb thirty years ago.

During the two years I had close contact with her, Isobel cared for eight or nine babies. I know it sounds extraordinary, and it is, but every one of them became well enough to be accepted for adoption. Two cases, a deaf baby and a blind baby, I clearly recall being pronounced incurable by medical specialists, yet both were healed. Simple but intelligent in her theology,

Isobel was not given to miraculous explanation. She said the only miracle was love, God's love flowing through her, as a channel, to the babies. Her explanation was that 'her babies' failed to see, hear or grow properly because they felt rejected and unloved. 'Love,' she would say, 'releases their will to live and be.'

In spite of her poverty and personal disadvantages, Isobel had an overwhelming sense of God's love for her. She was quite frank and honest about herself and would say, 'I am ugly on the outside, but beautiful on the inside'. Her love flowed to all who knew her. A totally accepting person, she was free of censoriousness about other people's lives. She believed that only love changed people. I, the raw, newly graduated, newly ordained priest who supposedly knew the truth—but didn't know how or why he 'knew'—saw in Isobel the reason. Only love knows. Only love redeems.

Isobel's love was the love of Christ's inner-worldly mysticism. She spoke of God and Christ without jargon and had none of the trappings too often associated with a religious or churchy person. The Spirit of Christ passed to and from her soul as naturally as the air flowing in and out of her lungs. This is the naturalness Simone Weil commends as the only measure of true religion:

> When a man's way of behaving towards things and men, or simply his way of regarding them, reveals supernatural virtues, one knows that his soul is no longer virgin; it has slept with God—perhaps, even without knowing it, like a girl violated in her sleep. That has no importance; it is only the fact that matters.
>
> The only certain proof a young woman's friends have that she has lost her virginity is that she is pregnant. Otherwise, there is no proof—not even if she should talk and behave lewdly. Her husband may be impotent.

In the same way, if a soul speaks of God with words of faith and love, either publicly or inwardly, this is no proof either for others or for itself. It may be that what it calls God is an impotent being— that is to say, a false God, and that it has never really slept with God.

What is proof is the appearance of supernatural virtues in that part of its behaviour which is turned towards men.

The faith of a judge is not seen in his behaviour at church, but in his behaviour on the bench.[13]

In his philosopher–king letter to President Reagan, Patrick White wrote about a growth in a humility which evolves after sophisticated intellects have wrestled with their passions, self-hatred and despair in their search for truth.

He contrasted this humility, calling it 'a greater humility', with the humility that 'simple souls' are born with. There is an unwarranted arrogance in this view, an arrogance which assumes so-called 'simple souls' do not have their growth struggles, too; an arrogance which assumes the superiority of sophisticated intellects.

What White was really talking about was love, not humility. He wanted Reagan to visit Russia in order to see that Russians were fellow human beings and not the 'evil empire' of Reagan's rhetoric. He wanted Reagan to promote nuclear disarmament, not for the sake of universal humility, but for the sake of universal peace and love. Perhaps he chose the word 'humility' because 'love' might have sounded too sentimental for a modern-day Caesar. Perhaps he avoided 'love' for reasons we have traversed about his own life. But humility is merely the ante-chamber to the mansion of love.

If White had said 'love', not 'humility', his arrogance would have glared more openly. Who has ever noticed a greater love, or even a greater humility, among those with sophisticated intellects? If there is to be a greater love, then everyone, whether intellectually sophisticated or simple, must wrestle 'with their passions, self-hatred and despair in their search for truth'.

If the meaning of life is love not 42, theorems or explanations, then finding it does not depend on intellectual prowess— all may discover or fail to discover it. When dealing with theorems and explanations, sophisticated intellects have the advantage, but all are equal before love. In a secular society, where rational intelligence is placed at the top of the status pedestal of knowing, the gift— and it is but grace's gift— of a sophisticated intellect may prove a barrier to finding the meaning of life as love.

Rarely are sophisticated intellects naive, but can they make the spiritual journey to innocence? Love requires innocence.

10.

Three colours innocent

A path from naivety through complexity to simplicity

NAIVETY AND INNOCENCE ARE TWO WORDS OFTEN used synonymously and interchangeably. It should not be so. *Naivety* is a state of childishness: the state of a self which knows and understands neither its own complexity of person nor the complexity of the world. Naivety is living in the fog. Its love comes cheaply, like the love of a faithful dog for its keeper.

Innocence is a state of childlikeness: the state of a self which has come to know and understand both its own complexity of person and the complexity of the world but, nevertheless, loves simply as if it were naive. Innocence is living after the fog has cleared. Its love is costly, like the love of Christ.

✠ The innocence of Jesus Christ

In all of literature, I know of no consistently successful portrayal of an innocent person, except the portrayal of Jesus Christ in the Gospels. Shakespeare's Cordelia in *King Lear* is an innocent, but she is a palely painted figure compared with the strong brushstrokes of the Gospel portraits of Jesus Christ.

That the Gospels' four different authors should succeed to a degree where all others, by comparison, have failed persuades me, without being overly literalist, that these accounts are close reminiscences of the actual, historical person of Jesus. The real Jesus lies not far below the surface of their stories. Nothing less could explain their success, when other writers have so conspicuously failed.

One cannot read the Gospels and say of the Jesus portrayed in them, 'There is a naive man'. Anything but! Yet one can read them and say, 'There is an *innocent* man'. This same Jesus of the Gospels says:

> Truly I tell you, whoever does not receive the kingdom of God as a little child will never enter it.[1]

We can safely assume that this is intended to include 'sophisticated intellects' as well as the 'simple-minded'.

The meaning of life is journeying from naivety to innocence, an explorer's trek discovering ever-widening vistas of love. But it is no return to the Garden of Eden.

In the symbolism of that story, after Adam and Eve eat the forbidden fruit of the Tree of the Knowledge of Good and Evil, the Lord God tells them that they are but dust and to the dust they shall return. The Lord God then turns them out of the garden to till the ground from whence their life derives. They are prevented from returning to Eden because the Lord God has placed 'a sword flaming and turning' to bar their entry.

Adam and Eve's naivety is ended; henceforth, salvation lies not behind, but in front of them, in the journey to innocence. We are left with no doubt that this journey will encompass the sordid and the shocking, when their eldest son Cain murders Abel, his younger brother.

Not until the life of Christ does the world see what a truly innocent human being looks like. Appropriately, this man of love is named by Paul 'the last Adam':

> Thus it is written: 'The first man, Adam, became a living being'; the last Adam became a life-giving spirit. But it is not the spiritual that is first, but the physical, and then the spiritual. The first man was from the earth, a man of dust; the second man is from heaven. As was the man of dust, so are those who are of the dust; and as is the man of heaven, so are those who are of heaven. Just as we have borne the image of the man of dust, we will also bear the image of the man of heaven.[2]

In other words, the journey from naivety to innocence, from Eden through time and space to heaven, is a treading in the footsteps of Jesus Christ. But in a world of the sordid and the shocking, what does it mean to journey from naivety to innocence, to walk in Christ's footsteps?

Kryzstof Kieslowski is a Polish film director who fled the communist regime of his homeland to work in France. His film trilogy, *Three Colours Blue* (liberty), *Three Colours White* (equality) and *Three Colours Red* (fraternity), is one of the most poetic and profound explorations of the journey from naivety to innocence in modern art. Sadly and ironically, Kieslowski died of a heart attack the day I began writing this chapter.

✠ The path to innocence in *Three Colours Blue*

Three Colours Blue opens with a car accident in which Julie, the film's central character, is the sole survivor. Her only child Anna and her husband Patrice, a renowned composer who is working on 'The Song for the Unification of Europe', both die. In hospital, Julie tries to kill herself by taking a drug overdose, but cannot and spits out the tablets before swallowing. Physically recovered but mentally and spiritually tormented, she destroys the unfinished score of Patrice's song, abandons the marital mansion, rents a flat in Paris and, with deliberate single-mindedness, lives a life of total anonymity and isolation.

Each film of the trilogy portrays a scene where a very aged, arthritic, stooped and humped man or woman reaches painfully and awkwardly to place an empty bottle in a glass recycling bin. And in each film the chief characters are young adults, in their late twenties or early thirties, who still live in naivety's fog. The aged bottle recyclers represent eventual decay and death—but also, with their determined recycling, care for life. In *Blue*, Julie is so withdrawn and self-enclosed that she fails even to see the elderly woman's struggle to place the bottle in the bin.

From the window of her upstairs flat, Julie watches a man being brutally beaten in the street below. Momentarily, he escapes and bangs on Julie's door, seeking refuge from his pursuers. Julie does not open the door. She cannot reach out to anyone; she has no love to give; she is entirely withdrawn from life.

A boy at the scene of the car accident stole Julie's necklace. Overcome with guilt, he manages to track Julie down and return the necklace, which was a gift from Patrice. From the necklace's chain hangs a gold cross. Julie tells the boy she doesn't want it; he can keep it.

Thoughts of suicide return and Julie experiments with drowning herself in a pool. It is half-hearted. Afterwards, she reaches out to another person's pain for the first time. A street musician, whom she's heard playing a tune similar to her husband's work, is lying on the pavement ill or asleep. Julie enquires if he is okay. She pushes his flute case under his head for a pillow and he says to her, 'You always gotta hold on to something'.

Julie's ability to love begins to grow again. But now it is not the easy love of her previously protected and privileged bourgeois life. It is a love which takes in the sordid and the shocking.

A prostitute who occupies a flat adjacent to Julie's, whom the building's other tenants have tried to evict, in a desperate state rings Julie late at night from the dive where she performs live sex acts on stage. Julie goes to this seedy joint to comfort her. A television set is playing there and Julie watches an interview with her late husband's musical associate, Olivier. He has a copy of Patrice's unfinished score, which Julie destroyed, and says he is trying to complete the song.

Julie is furious. She and Olivier meet and he tells her that she alone has sufficient understanding of her husband's work to finish composing the song. She expresses anger and disinterest.

Through Olivier, Julie learns what all, apparently, except she knew—that Patrice had a mistress. She goes to the courthouse where the mistress works as a lawyer, follows her into the toilets and a confrontation takes place. Julie discovers the mistress is pregnant with Patrice's child. In conversation, they each realise that Patrice loved them both. He has praised Julie's essential goodness to the mistress, whom Julie observes is wearing a necklace identical to the one Patrice gave her.

Olivier, who lives alone and has loved Julie ever since he began to work with Patrice, continues to complete the song, but now Julie joins him, slowly taking over the task he cannot accomplish, but she can. Julie makes a gift of her former marital home to Patrice's lover, so that his son can be brought up there. As they work together to complete 'The Song for the Unification of Europe', Julie realises that she is in love with Olivier. We now hear the words of the song: they are the words of Paul's hymn of love in 1 Corinthians 13:

> If I have prophetic powers and understand all mysteries and all knowledge, but do not have love, I am nothing.

Kieslowski has applied these words to Europe and the nations as well as to the individual characters of his film.

At the time of the car accident and Patrice's death, Julie is in her early thirties, but she is still, like Irenaeus' Adam and Eve, a naive child. She possesses little person in her own right. She is simply the wife of a great and revered composer, whose funeral is relayed on national television. Her love for Patrice was naive. Everyone knew he had a mistress, except her. Patrice spoke of Julie and her goodness to his mistress, but not of the mistress to Julie.

If Julie is to grow as a person— to become a knowing, loving adult, which according to Irenaeus is the divine purpose— then she must enter the world of sin, complexity and suffering. She is sorely tempted to avoid that world by living in anonymous isolation or by suicide.

Simone Weil's 'necessary suffering' has befallen Julie through the loss of her husband and only child. Her refusal to receive back the stolen necklace, with its hanging cross, is Julie's Job-like, Jung-like challenge to God and life.

Her slow but sure recognition of the pain of others, together with Olivier's gentle, non-pushy, respectful love for her, draws her back into life's journey. Her own dawning love for Olivier, and her completion of Patrice's song, give Julie the confidence to emerge from the fog of naivety to live and love as an innocent. Liberty is love.

The words of Paul's hymn of love in 1 Corinthians 13, which

are also the words of Patrice's song, describe the love of Christ the innocent this way:

> Love is patient; love is kind; love is not arrogant or rude. It does not insist on its own way; it is not irritable or resentful; it does not rejoice in wrongdoing but rejoices in the truth. It bears all things, believes all things, hopes all things, endures all things.

✠ The failure to achieve innocence in *Three Colours White*

Such a love as this, a love which 'rejoices in the truth', does not exist in the marriage of hairdressers Karol (a Pole) and Dominique (French) in the second film of Kieslowski's trilogy, *Three Colours White* (equality).

Karol is a gawky dolt and a loser, an adult boy. Dominique, whom he professes to love, is suing Karol for divorce on the grounds of non-consummation, because since their marriage, but not before, he's been impotent. Bird droppings fall from the sky, fouling his shoulder as he arrives for the court hearing. When the proceedings are ended, Dominique removes a trunk containing all his possessions from her car, dumps it at his feet and, waving him a pretty and victorious goodbye, drives off.

With nothing to his name but the trunk, Karol attempts to withdraw funds from an automatic teller machine, but it swallows his card because Dominique has cancelled his authority to operate their account. Desolate, as night falls, Karol sits in the street on his trunk, wondering what to do. He watches the tortured efforts of an arthritic, stooped, humped old man attempting to place a bottle in a recycling bin. Karol offers no assistance; he treats the little drama as an entertainment, a stupid, amused grin across his face.

Remembering he has a key to Dominique's beauty salon, he sleeps the night there. Discovering him the next morning, Dominique, at first angry, shows more than a little interest when he indicates that he can 'get it up'. Despite the divorce proceedings, does she 'love' him? As they undress, his erection fails again. Dominique tells him to go. When he refuses, she sets fire to the shop's curtains, telling Karol every policeman in Paris will be after him for doing it.

Karol retreats into the Metro where he busks, pathetically playing Polish tunes on a paper-covered hair comb. A middle-aged, well-dressed drunken compatriot, Mikolaj, recognises the tunes. Mikolaj offers Karol a large sum of money if he will shoot a man he knows (actually it is Mikolaj himself) who wishes to commit suicide, but won't do it himself because of the ill effect it would have on his wife and family. The broke and despairing Karol says: 'He has a wife, children, money and he wants to die?'

Karol shows Mikolaj where Dominique lives. They see Dominique and a lover silhouetted against the bedroom window. Karol rings her from a nearby 'phone booth. Dominique answers the 'phone, says 'perfect timing' and Karol is left listening to her gasps and groans of orgasmic ecstasy as she makes love with her visitor.

Continuing the film's style of black humour, Karol returns to Poland locked in his trunk, which is booked on the plane as Mikolaj's luggage. Ever the loser, Karol's trunk is stolen by thieves from Warsaw airport. Discovering its useless contents, the thieves beat up Karol and abandon him at the edge of a garbage dump. A cheap plaster bust, which he purchased in Paris, of a woman resembling Dominique is broken in the foray. He manages to return to his old home, where he glues the bust back together, badly, and kisses it.

Karol gains employment with a money changer and his character begins to alter from naive fool to self-serving sneak. Pretending to be asleep, he overhears his boss scheming with a colleague about a property development to take place on cheap peasant farming land. Cheating his boss, Karol plies one of the peasant owners with vodka, swindling from him land which is central to the proposed development. As he shaves in the peasant's house the next morning, a picture of the Madonna and child reflects in the mirror from the wall opposite. For a fleeting moment, the image sparks his conscience, then quickly and with a self-satisfied smile, he continues shaving.

Eventually, Karol becomes a very rich man. From Warsaw, he 'phones Dominique, but she hangs up on him. He devises a way to get her to Poland and to get even with her (equality?). He makes a will, leaving her all his wealth, and arranges his own death, complete with a fake certificate and a cheaply purchased Russian corpse as his substitute.

Dominique travels to Warsaw for the funeral and to collect her legacy. Karol, watching from afar, observes tears roll down her cheeks at the graveside. Returning to her hotel, Dominique discovers Karol in her bed. He makes love to her aggressively and successfully. She responds enthusiastically. He says: 'You moaned louder than on the phone.'

Next morning, before Dominique is awake, Karol disappears. Dominique, now 'in love' again with her rich and sexually-able husband, desperately phones around trying to locate Karol. While she is still on the phone and, just as Karol had planned, the police arrive. Dominique is arrested and eventually convicted of his murder, all Karol's friends confirming the battered exhumed corpse as his.

Officially dead, Karol must now lead an underground life for fear of arrest. With a hint of bribed guards, Karol gains access to Dominique's prison. From the courtyard, he can see her, and she him, high up at the window of her cell. In sign language, Dominique gestures that she and Karol are now equal, that she loves him and, by pretending to place a ring on her finger, that they are married again. Standing in the prison yard, desolate as ever, a tear rolls down Karol's cheek and the film concludes.

Karol and Dominique are certainly equal: equally pathetic. They do have some knowledge of the complexity of the world, but in self-knowledge they are naive. Psychically, they are mere children, but wicked children bent on dominating or destroying each other. They don't love; they just have needs. If ever they are to learn anything about themselves, then only suffering could teach them.

Dominique is a kind of psychosexual sadist who is so taken up with her own needs that she is completely insensitive to the pain she causes Karol. Yet she is such a psychic child that to call her a 'psychosexual sadist' is to attribute to her a depth she does not possess. That lack of depth is her problem.

Karol is the same. He has opportunity to know himself— for example, through Mikolaj's desire for suicide (despite having everything Karol desires) or via the Madonna in the mirror (a symbol of virtue, exposing his own sin and guilt)— but he ignores. When he does begin to grow up, it is only to become a cheat and an avenger. But there is little self-knowledge even in his wickedness. His plan to get even punishes him as much as Dominique. Karol and Dominique's equality is loveless; it amounts to the childish game of 'if you get me, I'll get you'.

Irenaeus perceived God's purpose in a fallen world, of which sin, suffering and death are a part, as growth to adult maturity. But of the necessity to discern good from evil, he warned: 'If anyone do shun the knowledge of both kinds of things and the twofold perception of knowledge, he unawares divests himself of the character of a human being.'[3]

Though they are in their late twenties or early thirties, Dominique and Karol possess such slender moral insight that one feels they might descend back through childhood to unbirth as human beings. They remind me of those elderly people I have visited as a priest who have not ripened, but stayed green and hard. By refusal to face self-truth, they create themselves as cardboard characters.

At the end of the film, Dominique in gaol, Karol officially dead, that necessity of suffering which Simone Weil calls 'the order of the world' is upon them. They recognise that their equality is checkmate, not love. But will they taste their suffering fully? We are left wondering whether their self-inflicted suffering will become a journey to hell or to heaven. They are no longer naive, but neither are they innocent.

✠ The glory of innocence in *Three Colours Red*

Three Colours Red (fraternity) is Kieslowski's crowning achievement: a film that achieves the quality of a great work of art. The journey from naivety to innocence is touchingly, but non-sentimentally, explored. *Red* is profound, beautiful, joyous, but above all glorious. Appreciation of the film will be enhanced by some understanding of the mysticism of glory.

'Glory' is a word seldom used in ordinary speech today except on those few occasions when we wish to express satisfied wonderment—for example, when we say, 'Such a glorious sun-set!' or 'What glorious weather we are having!' But 'glory' is a key word in the spiritual vocabulary of Christ's religion. If 'holy' is the biblical word which comes nearest to saying what God actually is, then 'glory' is next closest.

Like 'holy', 'glory' is a difficult and teasing word to explain. It means something like the 'shining-ness' or 'being-ness' of God. It has a long mystical history. In the Old Testament story, when Moses descends from Mount Sinai after receiving the Ten Commandments, the people could not look on his face because it shone so brightly with God's reflected glory. The first-century biblical interpreters of Christ drew on this same mysticism of glory to explain Christ as God's self-revelation.

Paul, for example, teaches a complex mysticism of glory. If we accept God's grace, accept that God accepts us in spite of our sins, then, says Paul in Romans 5: 1–2: 'We have peace with God through our Lord Jesus Christ, through whom we have obtained access to this grace in which we stand; and we boast in our hope of sharing the glory of God.'

'Boast' is used ironically here because 'our hope of sharing the glory of God' is a *gift* of grace, not our own achievement. But for Paul, the Beatific Vision, the fulfilment of human life, is 'a sharing the glory of God'—a participation in the 'shining-ness' and 'being-ness' of the divine life.

Paul's mysticism of glory is not only anticipatory of future fulfilment, but is also a process of ongoing fulfilment in the present. Eastern Christianity is bolder than Western and speaks of this process as *deification*. Those who have accepted divine grace, says Paul, are in the process of being transformed from one degree of glory to another.

To explain this, he draws upon the story of Moses' shining face. Moses, he says, shone with God's glory when he received the commandments, but Christ, the bestower of grace, shines with even greater glory. Moses had to veil his face, because looking at it was too much for the people. It reminded them of their sin and guilt. But Christ unveiled God's grace, a new kind of shining-ness— a shining-ness of divine love, of forgiveness, not judgment. Thus we should, says Paul, deliberately gaze on God's glory in Christ so that we may shine with the divine shining-ness, and live our finite being-ness in the infinite being-ness of God:

> And all of us, with unveiled faces, seeing the glory of the Lord as though reflected in a mirror, are being transformed from one degree of glory to another; for this comes from the Lord, the Spirit.[4]

Karol and Dominique know nothing of a mysticism of glory. Appropriately, it is night when they see each other across the gaol courtyard. Darkness and distance separate them. Their mutual sin has estranged them so completely from glory that repentance and grace are their only hope of avoiding a life of living death.

By contrast, *Three Colours Red* portrays a love between its two central characters which mystically transforms them both from one degree of glory to another. It is impossible to put into words the mystical beauty of this film, because so much of its art and power lies in visual images, symbols and sublime music.

Joseph Kern, one of the two main characters, is anything but naive. He knows people to such a degree that his vision borders on supernatural seeing. In his late fifties or early sixties, Kern is a retired judge. Late in the film, we learn the reason for his early retirement. The only woman he's ever loved left him in his youth for another man. She and the other man went to live in England, where she eventually died. The now-widowed man returns to France, where he owned a construction company responsible for a building which collapsed, causing several deaths. His case came before Kern who, justly, convicted him and sent him to prison. It was all too much for the judge, who retired world-weary and cynical.

Valentine, the other main character, is a beautiful young model. She meets the judge when she brings to his home Rita, the judge's injured dog, whom Valentine has run over. We watch Valentine tenderly pick Rita up off the road and gently place her on her car's rear seat. Valentine is aghast when the judge shows no interest in the injured animal.

'Should I take it to a veterinarian?' she asks.

'As you wish,' replies the judge.

'If I ran over your daughter, would you be so indifferent?' Valentine retorts.

'I have no daughter, Miss. Go away!' is his cold response.

Kern is not naive, but he is cynical, bitter, misanthropic and totally reclusive. Valentine is morally outraged when she discovers that he spends his days listening in on other people's telephone conversations via a large and sophisticated array of electronic eavesdropping devices. Through one of the loudspeakers, Valentine and the judge listen as a married male neighbour with a teenage daughter converses intimately with his homosexual lover. Valentine voices her disgust at such eavesdropping.

Kern invites her to go to the neighbour's house and tell him of Kern's crime. She does go, is warmly welcomed at the house by a generous-spirited wife, and sees that the neighbour's daughter is also eavesdropping on her father's upstairs conversation on a downstairs phone. Valentine retreats, says nothing about Kern, and excuses herself as having come to the wrong house. Life is more sordid, shocking and complex than her naive do-goodery imagined.

Back at the judge's house, Kern excuses his eavesdropping to Valentine by saying it is the only way to know the truth about people's lives. Recalling his years as a judge, he says:

> I don't know whether I was on the good side or the bad side. Here, at least I know where the truth is. My point of view is better than a courtroom.

The judge points to a window through which another neighbour can be seen walking in his garden, speaking on a mobile phone. He tells Valentine that this man is one of Europe's biggest heroin suppliers and invites her to ring him. Momentarily forgetting her disgust at Kern's misuse of the telephone, she rings the trader saying, 'You deserve to die'. Looking about him anxiously, the heroin trader runs into the security of his house.

Valentine does genuinely love. Heedless of Kern's unconcern for Rita, Valentine takes the dog to a veterinarian at her own expense, in the process discovering that Rita is expecting pups. Kern is a knower of knowers, but loveless. A turning point in the story is this conversation:

> 'Why did you pick up Rita?'
> 'Because I'd run over her. She was bleeding.'
> 'Otherwise you'd have felt guilty. You'd have dreamt of a dog with a crushed skull.'
> 'Yes.'
> 'So who did you do it for?'

There are, we feel, two opposite answers to the judge's question and both are correct: she did it for the love of the dog and she did it for the love of herself, not the dog. The first is Valentine's naive answer. The second is the judge's cynical answer. At this point, neither of them knows the love of innocence.

Valentine leaves Kern's house full of anger and disgust, but saying she pities him. His knowingness registers her disgust and this, together with the simplicity of her naive love, has touched his hardened heart. Immediately, he writes to the authorities informing them of his illegal 'phone tapping. Eventually, his case is heard in court and reported in the newspapers. Valentine sees the newspaper report and calls at Kern's house, ardently explaining that she had not turned him in. He tells her that he did it himself.

From this scene on, a deep platonic love begins to grow between the beautiful young model and the unkempt old judge. They drink pear brandy together, a love eucharist. She asks why he informed on himself. He says, 'You asked me to'.

Valentine posts Kern an invitation to a spectacular, glamorous fashion parade in which she is modelling. For the first time in years, the judge dresses well, grooms himself and goes out socially. After the parade, they sit alone amidst a sea of red seats in the fashion parade hall. Outside a storm rages.

He tells her of the first dream he's experienced for a long time. In it, he sees Valentine aged fifty with a man she loves deeply. But now she is a knower, too, and tells him things about the woman he once loved that he has not told her.

'How do you know all this?' he asks.

'It wasn't hard to guess,' she replies ironically. Kern's sharp observation and his intuition about people have become hers, too.

Valentine escorts the judge to his car. As he drives away, she notices an arthritic, stooped, humped elderly woman painfully trying to put a bottle in a recycling bin. The beautiful young Valentine assists her.

This summary of the story of *Red* is a bland simplification. The film itself is full of haunting, mystical images, symbols and music. There is a criss-crossing of people's lives and coincidental happenings and meetings of the Jungian synchronicity type.

In a subplot, the judge's earlier life is relived with striking parallels by a young judge who is destined to marry Valentine. This young judge has a girlfriend who jilts him. Kern has eavesdropped on their conversations. Kern realises that this girl-friend is a shallow character, who reminds him of the woman who left him in his youth. Meeting Valentine has shown him his lost love was not a true love at all. Compared with Valentine, she was faithless and hollow.

There are suggestions, never overasserted, that Kern is in touch with some mystical force that will draw Valentine and the young judge together, thus healing Kern's own tragic life and saving a repeat of it in the life of the young judge. In this and many other parts of the film, Kieslowski explores the borders between the world of everyday rational consciousness and another more real, more spiritual reality interconnected with it.

At the end of the film, a ferry carrying Valentine across the channel from France to England is overturned in a storm. Kern had persuaded her to take it and not to travel by air. We see Kern in his house playfully fondling Rita's pups. He watches news of the ferry disaster on television. It reports that of the fourteen hundred-plus passengers, only seven are known to have survived. Six of these are: Julie and Olivier (*Blue*), Dominique and Karol (*White*), Valentine and the young judge (*Red*). The news report also tells of the death, in the same storm, of a young couple on a yacht— the young judge's girlfriend and her new lover.

I said that Joseph Kern was not naive. About other people and the complexity of the world, that is true. But through his relationship with Valentine, he has discovered a profound naivety about his image of his lost love. He realises that he has lived to old age in a web of self-woven fantasy about a woman with whom he would never have found happiness.

Idealisation of her, and self-indulgence of the hurt she caused him, is the root source of his bitterness and cynicism. He is incapable of making love's journey until that fog of naivety lifts to reveal self-truth. Valentine's naive but genuine love is Kern's fog-dissipating sunshine. At the end of the film, Kern's tender handling of Rita's pups shows him displaying the love of an innocent.

At the beginning of the film, Valentine's gentle lifting of the injured Rita from the road touches us with the simplicity of her love. But this Valentine is Eve the child. She has not yet tasted the fruit of the Tree of the Knowledge of Good and Evil. Cruelly, Kern reveals the mixture of her motives in saving Rita.

Her simplistic do-goodery is exposed by the complexity of relationships in the homosexual neighbour's home. When Valentine phones the heroin trader and anonymously threatens him, she has stooped to the level of Kern's voyeuristic knowing. She has tasted the forbidden fruit. Valentine discovers that love, in the sordid and the shocking real world, is not always what the naive and the self-righteous take it to be. Near the end of the film, when she assists the old lady to deposit the bottle in the recycling bin,

Valentine has begun to love as an innocent.

By facing self-truth, where each has become a mirror to the other, Valentine, the young and gorgeous model, and Kern, the old and tatty judge, are drawn into a love which redeems them both: one from sentimentality, the other from cynicism. Both now have the potential to journey further into innocence and be transformed from one degree of glory to another. But their journey will continue to be a journey through the world of the sordid and the shocking, where love is the only transforming power. Fraternity is love.

Watching the scene in which Valentine and Kern's love is celebrated with a communion of pear brandy evoked in my memory a painful, personal trial of love.

During the mid-1980s, I helped a devout Muslim friend, a highly educated scientist who completed his doctoral studies in Australia, get his family back to Australia from Iran. Though practising Muslims themselves, as people with Western contacts and Western education, they were in danger from the Iranian fundamentalist regime.

During a critical period of the immigration negotiations, my friend spent a few days staying at our home in Canberra. He came with me one morning to the theological college where I was the principal. He asked to attend the morning chapel service, which happened that day to be a eucharist. As staff and students were receiving the bread and wine, symbols of Christ's sacrifice of love, he nudged me and asked if he could receive, too.

My mind raced with the theological issues. I thought, 'Anglicans offer open communion to all Christians of any denomination, but a Muslim? Can a person who respects Jesus Christ as God's prophet, but not as God incarnate, receive communion?'

I had never faced these issues in theory, but now I was faced with them in total, practical immediacy by a dear friend in deep pain about his family.

'What is the eucharist?' I asked myself. 'Surely, it is a sacramental channel of God's love and a sharing of that love with each other,' I answered myself. 'Can you exclude someone from a channel of God's love because they don't have the right beliefs?' one voice within me asked. 'What will the staff or other bishops think?' enquired another. 'He wants to participate, it is his choice, there is no coercion of any kind,' my thoughts went on.

All this occurred within the space of about sixty seconds. I whispered in his ear 'yes', and he received the sacrament of bread and wine. To my surprise and delight, no member of staff or any student later disagreed with this decision. Love is always innocent.

Yesterday, as I write, the *Sydney Morning Herald* published an obituary on the life of Kryzstof Kieslowski (1941–1996). Describing Kieslowski 'as among the greatest of contemporary film-makers', and saying that his death robs 'us of one of cinema's last, best hopes', its author, Shane Danielson, continued:

This question— of what was real, what mattered most— appeared to preoccupy him in his final years and allowed his inner conflict full rein. He would at one moment dismiss his achievements as 'meaningless, utterly irrelevant to the real world'— yet, in the next, confess how deeply he was moved by the letter of a fourteen-year-old girl, shortly after the release of *The Double Life of Veronique*, who claimed that film, more than any other piece of evidence, had finally convinced her of the existence of the human soul.

'That one letter,' he admitted, 'made everything I have done worthwhile.'[5]

What is real? What matters most? At the end of his life, before his premature death, I think Kieslowski knew. He did not merely believe— he knew.

Endnotes

Chapter 1

1. David Marr (ed.), *Patrick White Letters*, Random House, Australia, 1994, p.345
2. Patrick White, *Flaws in the Glass*, Jonathan Cape, London, 1981, p.144
3. *Ibid*, p.67
4. *Ibid*, p.145
5. *Ibid*
6. *Patrick White Letters*, p.363
7. Monica Furlong, *Merton: A Biography*, Collins, London, 1980, pp.55–56
8. *Ibid*, p.71
9. *Ibid*, p.77
10. Galatians 1: 13–16
11. Acts 9: 1–9
12. William James, *The Varieties of Religious Experience*, Collins, London, 1960, p.190

Chapter 2

1. *Patrick White Letters*, p.363
2. *Ibid*, p.208
3. Colin Wilson, *Beyond the Outsider*, Pan Books, London, 1972, p.225
4. *The Varieties of Religious Experience*, pp.373–374
5. *Beyond the Outsider*, p.164
6. *Ibid*, p.165

7. C.G. Jung, *Memories, Dreams, Reflections*, Collins, London, 1977, pp.333–334

Chapter 3

1. Sigmund Freud, *New Introductory Lectures on Psychoanalysis*, Penguin Books, England, 1973, p.140
2. *Patrick White Letters*, p.361
3. *Flaws in the Glass*, pp.129–130
4. *Patrick White Letters*, p.363
5. Mark 3: 20–21
6. Mark 3: 31–35
7. *Flaws in the Glass*, p.154
8. *Ibid*, p.70
9. Matthew 21: 23–27
10. Luke 7: 31–35
11. *Flaws in the Glass*, pp.187–188
12. Proverbs 7: 22–24 and 29–36

Chapter 4

1. Aldous Huxley, *The Collected Works of Aldous Huxley*, Chatto & Windus, London, 1972, p.12
2. R.C. Zaehner, *Mysticism: Sacred and Profane*, Oxford University Press, London, 1961, p.209
3. *Ibid*, pp. 209–210
4. *The Varieties of Religious Experience*, p.374
5. 1 Corinthians 13: 1–2
6. 1 Corinthians 13: 8–12
7. *The Collected Works of Aldous Huxley*, p.58
8. *Patrick White Letters*, p.90
9. *Ibid*, p.409
10. *Ibid*, p.196
11. Bertrand Russell, *Why I Am Not a Christian*, Simon & Schuster, New York, 1967, pp.115–116
12. *Flaws in the Glass*, p.68
13. Romans 1: 19–20

14. *Patrick White Letters*, p.237
15. Isaiah 6: 1–8

Chapter 5

1. *Patrick White Letters*, p.591
2. *Flaws in the Glass*, pp.182–183
3. William McGuire and R.F.G. Hull (eds), *C.G. Jung Speaking*, Pan Books, London, 1980, p.122
4. *Ibid*, p.121
5. Luke 23: 39–43
6. *Sydney Morning Herald*, 23 March 1996
7. Leonardo Boff, *St Francis*, SCM Press, Great Britain, 1985, p.146
8. *Ibid*
9. *Ibid*, p.147
10. *Ibid*, p.148
11. Act 2, scene 2
12. Act 3, scene 1

Chapter 6

1. Mark 3: 28–29
2. *C.G. Jung Speaking*, p.383
3. *Memories, Dreams, Reflections*, p.52
4. *Ibid*, p.55
5. *Ibid*
6. *Ibid*, pp.56–57
7. *Ibid*, p.57
8. *Ibid*, p.59
9. Job 1: 10–11
10. Job 1: 20–22
11. Job 2: 4–5
12. Job 2: 9–10
13. Job 3: 3–4, 11–12, 16 and 23
14. Mark 15: 34
15. Job 40: 2

16. Job 40: 4
17. Job 42: 1–6
18. Job 42: 7–8

Chapter 7

1. John Hick, *Evil and the God of Love*, Macmillan, London, 1966, p.218
2. *Ibid*, p.219
3. *Ibid*, p.220
4. *Ibid*, p.221
5. Peter L. Berger, *A Rumour of Angels*, Penguin Books, England, 1971, p.84
6. *Ibid*, p.85
7. *Ibid*, pp.87–89
8. Dietrich Bonhoeffer, *Letters and Papers from Prison*, Collins, Great Britain, 1959, p.100
9. *Ibid*, p.118
10. C.G. Jung, *Answer to Job*, Routledge & Kegan Paul, London, 1979, p.86

Chapter 8

1. *Flaws in the Glass*, pp.251–252
2. *Patrick White Letters*, pp.603–604
3. *Ibid*, p.616
4. *Flaws in the Glass*, p.102
5. *Ibid*, p.12
6. *Patrick White Letters*, p.550
7. 1 John 4: 7–12
8. 1 John 4: 16–18
9. Romans 8: 31–39

Chapter 9

1. *Patrick White Letters*, p.363
2. Clifton Woltens (trans.), *The Cloud of Unknowing*, Penguin Books, England, 1961, pp.57–58
3. *Ibid*, pp.53–54

4. David McLellan, *Simone Weil: Utopian Pessimist*, Papermac, London, 1991, p.137
5. *The Cloud of Unknowing*, p.55
6. *Patrick White Letters*, p.363
7. *Ibid*
8. *The Cloud of Unknowing*, p.58
9. *Patrick White Letters*, p.363
10. George A. Panichas, *The Simone Weil Reader*, David McKay Company, New York, 1977, p.465
11. *Ibid*, p.450
12. *Ibid*, p.451
13. *Ibid*, p.429

Chapter 10
1. Mark 10: 35
2. 1 Corinthians 15: 45–49
3. *Evil and the God of Love*, p.220
4. 2 Corinthians 3: 18
5. *Sydney Morning Herald*, 18 March 1996

STREETS OF HOPE
Finding God in St Kilda

Tim Costello

Lunching in public with a prostitute is not the way most
Baptist pastors begin their ministry—but the Reverend
Tim Costello is not like most.

After theological training in pristine Switzerland, Tim
Costello's first ministry was in St Kilda—a waterfront
suburb of Melbourne as famous for its sex and drugs and
'no-hopers' as for its ethnic mix and cosmopolitan
cultures. *Streets of Hope* is his warm and personal story of
this formative time: the encounters and characters, the
challenges to his skills as a lawyer, to his convictions as a
churchman, to ideas and values—about family, sex and
spirituality, caring and charity, the law and the
powerless, the need for community in an age of
insecurity.

In his writing and public speaking the Reverend Tim
Costello seeks a vision for national morality—a republic
with a conscience—and shows the power the church can
have as champion of the common good.

ISBN 1 86448 890 5